Buddhist
to
Catholic

~

from Zafu to Kneeler

by

Patricia Masters

ContemplativeChristians.com

ContemplativeChristians.com Publishing
First Printing. November 2017
Austin, TX

Library of Congress Cataloging-in-Publication Data

Masters, Patricia
Buddhist to Catholic: From Zafu to Kneeler
ISBN 13: 978-0-692-96168-1

Printed in the United States of America.

Cover art by Brian Burrowes.

Thanks be to God. Thanks to everyone who encouraged me to write this story, and who gave their time and energy to review and critique my efforts.

This book is dedicated to
Bernadette Roberts, in gratitude.

"Ask and it will be given to you; seek and you will find; knock and the door will be opened to you. For everyone who asks receives; he who seeks finds; and to him who knocks, the door will be opened."

~Matthew 7:7-8

Contents

Introduction

In this modern age when it is possible to read esoteric works formerly hidden and secret, and to meet teachers from every tradition, it is not unusual for people to shop among and even change religions, or create their own.

Most commonly, we hear how someone raised in the Catholic Church leaves it for the supposedly deeper wisdom of the Eastern traditions. If my life is unusual in any way, it may only be that the journey took me in the opposite direction – from Hinduism to Buddhism, and in the end, to Catholicism, my true and final spiritual home. Perhaps it is unusual as well in the number and variety of opportunities that came my way and in the meetings and help I received along the way. Books, teachers and friends appeared just ahead on the path like bread crumbs leading home. It is only in retrospect that one sees God's hand in it; every spiritual journey is made up of God's graceful action and our response to it.

This is the story of a plain person, told in a plain way. If it is too long in places, I apologize for that. There may be paragraphs or even chapters you'll want to skim over.

Believe me I cut it and cut it until I got so tired of rereading it that I could not face it one more time. As a neophyte writer I beg the reader's patience and understanding. At its best this story should be an encouragement, confirming that the grace and power of God is available, full-force, to everyone. And secondly, that the desire we have to know the Truth is *already* our connection to God, and forms our path.

It was hard to get started writing this story because it is difficult to write about how God's grace unfolded in my life without ending up pointing to myself and the somewhat interesting life I've lived. For example, along with many others, I experienced and participated in the wildness of the 1960's, practiced some years in the Hindu and then Buddhist tradition with well-known teachers, even spent ten years in a cult with AdiDa Samraj, the American guru. It was an interesting life because it was an interesting time. But it was also full of errors and worse. Fortunately, God reached out and redirected me again and again, bringing me home to the Catholic Church and, most of all, to the Eucharist. In earlier efforts to write about that journey, I often found myself side-tracked into stories of the travels, the people and the unusual experiences – taking me far from the point. Nonetheless I persevered, in response to an urge to share what was most precious to me.

I have wondered why an ordinary person born into a nominal Protestant family, should be led through the Eastern traditions and into the Catholic Church. What ideas and experiences led to that choice? Or as others have put it, *What were you thinking?!* What I will try to do here is to answer that for myself, as well as for any others who might be interested.

In hindsight, I can say that being inundated with different points of view is not helpful and in fact can be very detrimental. Whatever religion or philosophy we decide to practice, I've learned that it is imperative to stick to one path alone. Jumping around, allowing the ego to create its own path from bits and pieces of others will keep the ego in charge and looking good, while keeping God out. That is the fast track to nowhere, or a needlessly long and winding path to the goal.

In this time and place of abundant choice, the eclectic approach may sound ecumenical, but it has never produced significant results – not to my knowledge at least. At some point we must put aside all thoughts about the contemplative life and just live it. We must be patient and keep in mind the slogan: *Nothing in it for me,* or as St. John of the Cross wrote: *All for Thee, nothing for me*. But, as I said, that was something I came to understand only years later. Now I will tell the story as it was, without that insight.

Looks Like Lost

In 1994, while living at a Zen training center in Northern California, a well-known Roshi came to visit. He arrived at the Center much later than expected. After greeting him, we went into the Zendo. The Roshi took his seat and began speaking, first telling the story of why he was late. He said that though they were given a map, somehow the instructions were not clear to the driver and four different times on the journey they had to stop and ask for clarification and direction. Finally, a considerate postman led them to the Zen Center in his truck. After relating his story, the Roshi paused for a moment, then said, *Looks like lost, but… just went another way*.

The Roshi's wisdom-saying is a fitting preface for my own journey. Looking back over my meandering spiritual path, I certainly must have *looked like lost* many times, unsure where I was going or what was guiding and motivating me. Until I understood the questions I was trying to answer and what was leading me, my journey looked a bit like a plastic bag on a windy day – up there, over there, swirling around, then getting stuck on a branch, and then off again.

At the time, I did not realize that the various teachings and experiences I was exploring were coming directly from God, regardless of what seemed to be their source. I did not see the journey as all of a piece, a whole woven from the parts, nor did I see the guiding Hand that led me.

This book was originally named *Looks Like Lost*, however in the hope of reaching anyone who might have been on a similar journey, the name was changed to *Buddhist to Catholic*.

The Journey Begins

"To arrive at that which you know not, you must go by a way that you know not."[1]

I seem to have been born with the awareness that being alive is a mystery. From the time that I could think about it, I wanted to find the real, underlying truth of what life is; what I am and how it all fits together. How does everything exist? What is it? What am I? What is it to be an I?

I asked these existential questions (what my parents called *strange* questions) from an early age – questions for which it seemed no one had an answer or even an interest. My family was not religious, nor regular church goers. They never prayed or mentioned God and so I knew nothing about what such a thing could be. What I did know was that being alive, having suddenly appeared in this world, was mysterious;

---

[1] *St. John of the Cross, Ascent to Mt. Carmel, XIII.*

being able to think and to perceive of myself and the world around me – what was that?

Where did that ability come from? I would wave my hands around the room, the sky, the ground and ask my parents, *What is this?,* meaning why are we here, what are we for, what is the world, what am I, and so on. No one gave me an answer except to discourage me from asking such questions. They'd say things like, *don't think about those things,* and my mother warned, *you'll go crazy if you do.*

At about age seven, lying in bed one night I noticed a steady thumping noise. The next day I asked my father about it and he told me it was my heart beating. *And what is that; what makes the noise?,* I asked. He explained some basics – the blood pumps into the heart and then is pumped out again, leading to the noise.

I pressed further. *But what made it pump the first time?* He just shook his head and, most likely, went back to his newspaper. I recall that another frequent question of my childhood mind was, *Why am I me and not somebody else?* Self-awareness, consciousness, was perhaps the most mysterious thing of all to me. I thought it likely that adults already knew the answers and it was one of those things I would learn later. I quickly recognized that this was not the case.

As a child I spent a lot of time wandering off alone, often up the hill at the end of our street to the fields of a Franciscan Seminary. Just inside the wire fence was a giant oak tree. Taking my seat among its spreading roots and pressing my back against it, I would gaze at the fields and the sky, at the clouds and the few cows that wandered in the grass.

There seemed to be Something in the *background* – with me all the time – but that could not be seen for the looking. I was aware of It, and the trees and ground and sky, in their silence and stillness, seemed to be aware of It too.

The *Something* was a mystery and it formed the Background to all life. I thought that if I could just get still enough, I might see and experience this mystery clearly, perhaps even pass into It in some way. How to do this seemed to me to be of utmost importance.

Because my family was not religious, they did not offer me the standard Christian answers. They did not tell me about God and God's creation, about being a soul and God's plan for me.

And, I'm grateful that they did not. My home life, like millions of others, sadly, was made difficult due to alcoholism. Perhaps if I had been given answers and then pointed toward the Protestant Church (the only possibility for me in my circumstance at that time), I would have grasped at the security it offered, clung to it and denied the need for my own answers. Instead I had to put it together myself from my own perceptions, from what I now know as God's silent help expressed in Nature, through my experiences in the nearby Seminary field and eventually from books. This intuition of the mystery of existence, and my own curiosity was God's way, of calling someone who did not even know God's name.

Every day on the long walk to and from school I passed by a Carmelite convent. The singing and alternating silence coming from the monastery's chapel drew my attention. I questioned a friend, a little girl who was Catholic, about what they were doing in there and she said they were called nuns and they spent the whole day being quiet and talking to God. I ran home very excited because now I knew what I wanted to be – a nun!

That would be my opportunity to spend all day exploring this Background silence without interruption. However, when I told my plan to my mother she said, *You can't be a nun because we are not Catholic!* I responded, *Then I want to become Catholic.*

She said that was not possible, as one had to be *born Catholic – like Italians*, meaning – we are not Catholic and so neither can you be. On hearing this (and taking it as law the way children do), I felt a shock of disappointment, as if a giant door had been slammed in my face. Though I was powerless to change it, that did not change my intention. I continued to spend time alone in nature and they were profound times.

The Silent Presence which introduced Itself to me there coupled with an ongoing sense of mystery nurtured the search in which I would spend much of my adult life.

Since the door to the Catholic Church had seemingly closed, I began to develop my own cosmology, a way of understanding my place in the world that stayed with me, albeit unconsciously, for many years.

How I put it all together was that there was an ever-present, silent, all-encompassing *Something* which was the Background to all existence, with me (and everyone else, I assumed), at all times. I could never manage to focus on it, nonetheless it was always there, like an unending hum at the edge of awareness.

It seems that most of life and attention is given to the Foreground, where we live our lives. And I never gave much thought to what might be called the middle-point, the self, the dividing line and the door (or obstruction) between the two. Though these ideas were simplistic, the cosmology developed at this young age directed my spiritual path well into adulthood, though I did not see that fact until I sat down to write this story.

Where did these questions come from and why did I have them? I am sure now it was an intuition of the Divine and a gift from God. Initially, I had the questions and a mystifying sense of existence; then came the magnetic silence I met in Nature.

I had no person and no religion to explain all this to me, and as I said, I am glad for that. The quality of explanations I would most likely have received then might have stopped me from questioning further and searching more deeply. Even had I been able to join the Catholic Church at that time perhaps, I would have settled for the security of replacing mystery with doctrine. Looking back on those early years, I see God stirring the waters of my life and setting me off on the path.

Later in high school I read everything in the school library on religion, spirituality, and especially anything about miracles and exotic spiritual experiences, all in the service of answering my own questions.

Miracles seem to confirm that something is going on here. I bought a rosary and tried to teach myself how to pray with it. My father told me that his mother and her family had been Catholic but had left the Church before he was born due to a disagreement about where my great-grandfather could be buried.

Nothing in the Protestant Christian culture in which I lived was of interest to me; it did not seem to be focused on or even indicate awareness of the Abiding Presence that had informed my early years.

By the time I graduated high school in 1962, Eastern and Indian culture and religion appeared to be the rage with young people in America. Even in Kansas, where I grew up, Hindu gurus and yogis began to visit and I never missed the opportunity to hear them speak and, when possible, to question them.

In order to be able to pursue these interests I knew I had to get away from home, which was not an easy thing for an eighteen-year-old, working-class girl to do. Girls in my area were culturally divided into three groups: rich girls went to college, bad girls lived on their own and did whatever they wanted, and poor, good girls stayed home and got married young.

Being of the third group, I got married at eighteen, primarily so I could get out on my own. A year later my husband and I had a son, and eight years after that we were divorced.

All during that time I continued to read anything I could find on spirituality, even some of the more fringe subjects. One influential book was *There is a River,*[2] the story of the sleeping prophet, Edgar Cayce. Cayce's reading on the creation of mankind had a strong impact on me. It seemed to provide an explanation, a bridge between the scientific and spiritual world views. As I read it, I became so filled with energy and excitement that I was up all that night in a kind of ecstatic state.

It was confirmation that there were other Westerners interested in the same questions. Maybe I would be able to find others with answers. Because of my circumstance and environment, the only spiritual organizations I knew of were Protestant churches. So the next day I went to one nearby, an American Baptist church, and asked to be baptized. Because I was obviously very fervent and serious, they agreed. I joined the church and tried to participate fully, even teaching Sunday school and once giving a talk to the congregation.

Little by little though, it dawned on me that I did not fit in. No one seemed interested in asking the kind of questions that attracted me. I was even asked

---

[2]Thomas Sugrue.

to stop teaching Sunday school because I didn't stay closely within the dictates of the official curriculum. After a year I just drifted away through disinterest, and they were most likely glad to see me go.

No longer interested in Christianity, at least in the kind I had encountered in the church, I returned to studying the Eastern Religions. I read the *Gospel of Ramakrishna* and signed up for his correspondence course. I tried to meditate as they taught and also learn yoga. Later, I took initiation in Transcendental Meditation and went to California for a retreat with Maharishi Mahesh Yogi.

I met the yogi Satchadananda and began meditating and practicing yoga at a local Vedanta Temple. My friends called me *the method of the month girl*, and they were right. I was not willing to ignore any opportunity, and the more exotic, the better. I was looking for the true path, the right path.

Some years later, divorced and supporting myself and my son, I began to attend the local university, majoring in religion. It was not easy to get an in-depth look at Eastern religions – or even Catholic mysticism

– at a Bible-belt university, but at least now I had access to the university library. My term papers were frequently returned with a note like, *Unusual point of view* or *not what was asked for*. I was reading and writing to answer my own questions, rather than the professors'!

Things progressed until, walking around campus one day, reading a Buddhist Sutra, I spontaneously dropped into an altered state of awareness in which the Oneness of everything revealed itself. It was a powerful experience lasting two days.

The foreground had dissolved into the Background, of which everything was part. The experience was further confirmation and inspiration. What was made clear was that meditation techniques and spiritual reading had no control over that Oneness; It came of Its own accord. I summarily gave all my spiritual books away and stopped meditating. I had no idea what to do next but the urge was stronger than ever to find the Truth that Oneness had revealed.

Guru Story

I came across the first book of an American guru known at that time as Franklin Jones. Later he would change his name many times: from Bubba Free John to Da Free John, and with a few others in between, ending with Adi Da Samraj.

His first book was *The Knee of Listening*, partly an autobiography and partly a description of his spiritual experiences and what he understood or realized based on those experiences. Though I found the biography to be off-putting, when I arrived at the back of the book there was an essay entitled *The Way of Understanding*. This essay seemed a perfect description of my own experience of the Oneness. He wrote that the experience had become permanent in his case, so naturally I was interested. I immediately contacted his community and they sent me the manuscript of his second book, *The Method of the Siddhas*. I devoured this also and began a correspondence with someone in the community, a woman close to the Guru's inner circle.

Eventually she communicated *Bubba's* invitation to come and join them in California.

I was not really interested in having a guru so much as in finding a community which was living according to what was written in his books. I knew nothing about the role of gurus except that, in India, they were teachers of some kind. While that might be useful, being in the company of people who were pursuing the truth was what really attracted me. Though there seemed to be truth in what he had written of his experience, I was not really interested in the truth someone else found, only as I could know it myself.

When someone claims to have lived to fulfillment the same search you are on, you want to see them, see how they turned out and what they might have to say.

I made plans to move to California, tossed out or gave away most of my belongings, packed what was necessary and moved to California to join what was then known as the Dawn Horse Communion. I arrived at their headquarters in San Francisco in September 1974, and spent the next ten years in the community, much of it in close contact with the guru. My ten-year old son went with me, but it was only a few months before he asked to return home to live with his father.

The event of his leaving was without doubt the terrible price I paid to live in that community. I offer no excuse for letting him go except that at that time my priorities were – find God (a word with which I was becoming more comfortable), after that, personal life and relationships would take care of themselves.[3]

I was drawn to religion partly as a hoped-for cure for suffering. The Buddha said there were several reasons why people would begin spiritual practice – for love, for wisdom, and to end suffering. All my life I had experienced recurring dark moods in which a fog of physical, mental and emotional heaviness would descend for no apparent reason. Nothing alleviated it – until, again for no apparent reason and on its own time, it would just go away. This was troubling because I

---

[3] Though we kept in touch, it was close to fifteen years before my son Tim and I became close again. I'm grateful to be able to say that after those years we again formed a strong and loving bond. During the early years, Tim lived with his father in Kansas.

suffered from the New Age idea that spiritual seekers who are trying to live the right way should not get depressed.

The symptoms included bouts of sighing, crying, along with feelings of hopelessness and despair. At those times I tried to pray and read, usually in the hope of finding relief or at least some reason for what was happening but nothing really worked to ease it. I spoke to a doctor and she said perhaps there was a physical imbalance rather than a mental or emotional condition and suggested I take prescription medicine for it. I never considered doing that because I did not understand enough about the drugs and their effect on consciousness to take a chance.

I felt I needed to keep my awareness as natural as possible to be available to the working of the Divine. Plus even then I knew that if this difficulty came to me it must be for my benefit, and the best way of dealing with it was to try to understand or come up with a reason for it, though the years would teach me that knowing *why* is no guarantee of relief.

I had the intuition that the most efficacious thing might be to just bear it, stay in place, possibly without understanding it at all. I was encouraged by what I read in Zen books, that the best and the toughest practice is being willing to continue with "*No gain and no understanding*", or what I would now call just going on Faith.

Though this story is not about the Da Free John experience (others have already written about that) I want to share how I spent the years with Da Free John, and how his community both helped and hindered my spiritual journey.

What was best about that life was the opportunity to live an ordered and centered existence with daily time marked out for meditation, study, exercise and service. Information and instruction focused on meditation, yoga, eating in a healthy manner, keeping one's house in order and having harmonious relationships. There was in-depth consideration of personal relationships and one's own personal psychology. I learned to understand and get along with all kinds of people, learned about myself and what I was up to, my hidden agendas. To this day I still find myself using and sharing the wisdom that I gained from Adi Da and the life in his community.

What hindered, was the degree to which we were constantly involved in the drama created by the teacher and how little time and opportunity there was for silence, solitude or meditation. As soon as one began to go through some episode that might lead to personal self-understanding and growth, it would be disrupted by the guru or his minions, spiraling off into more exciting and sometimes terrifying guru-drama.

As the years in the community went by I found that I could no longer access the inner desire for God that had set me on the path to begin with. I could no longer discern what was right and good for myself – without asking the teacher or the community members. My own discrimination and intention were no longer available.

Seemingly I had made the choice to allow the guru to get between me and God. The community life was all-encompassing and highly insular. We were with each other and focused on the guru 24/7 – so much so that I could not have told you who was president during those years. Between the drama and the demanding schedule, the world – including one's family and friends – were forgotten.

The whole thing fell apart one day when Steve, my former husband and my son's father, contacted me to tell me that his brother had died. Steve and I had a chilly relationship at the time, and yet there he was, clearly calling for support and sympathy.

As I listened to him, at first, I felt absolutely nothing except a mild dismissive feeling, that *these people* were *in the world*, living *unlawful lives* and *outside the truth* (guru-speak) and so what happened to them didn't matter all that much. As soon as these thoughts had formed, instantly there was a *shock,* and in a flash I saw things as if I were standing outside myself. After ten years of spiritual practice did I have no other response to someone who needed comfort? A voice in my mind said, *Is this how you thought you would be after ten years in a spiritual community?* Instantly I dropped my cool attitude and offered Steve what comfort I could. Then I hung up the phone and packed up and left the community.

I went to stay with my father and his wife in Hawaii, to have time and space to think and to be as far from my former life as possible. Somehow my search had gone wrong and I had to get some distance from the whole thing.

At my father's home, as I unpacked my suitcase, I found that Dad had left a book on my nightstand, a book called *Snapping*,[4] which I read hungrily. And what I read told me that my experience of waking up or *snapping* out of it during that telephone call with Steve, is something that happens to many people who have lived in a cult. The snapping experience was a bit like waking up from a dream or coming out of hypnosis and realizing you are, and always have been, free.

The months that followed leaving the commune were full of chaos and confusion, doubt and fear. I had to find a way to live and work in a world to which

---

[4] Flo Conway and Jim Siegelman.

I had turned my back. For example, I was used to following dietary guidelines, yet I now hardly knew what to eat.

I was no longer sure when to get up or what to wear. At first, I tried continuing to follow the rules of the community but the further I got away from my time in the organization the less I wanted anything to remind me of it. At the same time, I felt the re-birth and intensification of my previous spiritual desire, but after ten years in the community I was clueless as to how and where to proceed. I certainly didn't want to join any more groups. I decided to spend a month or so in solitude and silence, trying to scrape the guru's name off my spirituality, find out what I knew to be true and what was just much repeated (and accepted) doctrine implanted I had acquired while in the group.

I went back to basics – sitting in silence and simply paying attention, trusting that God or Truth would guide me, and trying to find again that Mysterious Background that had first called me. Having been out of touch with my own discrimination and love of God, it took some time and silence for it to re-surface.

Just before I left the community Da Free John encouraged everyone to read *The Experience of No Self* by Bernadette Roberts. Though of course he did not consider her to be in his same high category of spiritual realization (no one could be), he had good things to say about her and about the book. The fact that she was an American and a woman interested me, though I had no interest in Christianity.

I bought the book and read it. The sensation was of having to stand on my intellectual and spiritual tippy-toes to grasp what was written and at the same time I had an intuition that Truth was there – I could sense it. I read the book several times while I was setting up my new life.

Around the same time, I met and became friends with Jack Kornfield, the Buddhist teacher, and began sitting meditation with his group, though also in no way interested in becoming a Buddhist. Buddhism was and is very popular in California, *the* thing to do. And I was most familiar and comfortable with spiritual seekers on the Eastern path.

At that same time I was also introduced to Zen teacher Jakusho (Bill) Kwong Roshi and his Zendo and community at Genjoji Training Center, where I also went to meditate. I loved the beauty and austerity of Zen. I was still healing from my experience in the community and though excited to be back on my own and feeling sure I had done the right thing in leaving the Free John group, I had no idea which direction to take.

Around that time a friend shared a quote by Carl Jung which said something to the effect that when a person becomes serious about spiritual life it is imperative to go back and make peace with one's cultural religion because one is still operating under the influence of the archetypes of that religion.

He said that for those raised in the United States, if every time we hear the words God or Jesus we feel anger or even revulsion, whatever new practice we take up will mostly be in argument with those early cultural archetypes. I have tried and failed to find this quote but actually it no longer makes any difference to me whether this is exactly what Jung wrote.

The value of it was that it gave me permission to explore Christianity and, in particular, Catholicism, for the first time since my early childhood attraction. Simultaneously I read the writings of Thomas Merton, Meister Eckhart, and Bernadette Roberts, though all the while practicing Buddhist meditation.

I spoke to Jack about my interest in Christianity and he gave me the name and address of someone he called *a little Catholic monk* whom he thought I could write to with my questions, a certain Fr. Thomas Keating. Completely unaware that Fr. Keating was well known and one of the originators of centering prayer, a Christian meditation practice, I began a correspondence with him.

After about six months I came upon a poster in a bookstore advertising an upcoming talk. The shocker was that the speaker was Fr. Thomas Keating! Beneath the notice was information about the books he'd written, his work with centering prayer, etc. This was my little monk! I was more than surprised but I sent him a letter telling him I would be at that event and we would get a chance to meet. Out of that meeting came an opportunity to attend a ten-day retreat with him at the Benedictine Monastery in Snowmass, Colorado.

While on that retreat, in a private conversation with Fr. Keating I had the first intimation of a personal relationship with Christ. In a period of private time alone with Fr. Keating, we sat talking and suddenly I had the strong sensation of someone else there with us. All my attention was drawn to that Presence. I wondered if I was feeling Father Keating's personal relationship to Christ. It was the first experience for me of what it means to say God is personal or to speak of a personal relationship with Christ. Later that night in the Chapel, when I heard the monks singing the Kyrie Eleison it was clearly a love song! They were singing to a Beloved *Someone.*

One always hears about a personal relationship with Christ – but I admit my understanding up to that point was more something like wearing a school sweater or waving a flag that said Jesus on it, than of an actual relationship that could be personally experienced. I was deeply affected and the mystery of it drew me. God as personal? Hmm. A new idea for me.

From 1985 – when I left the Da Free John community – to 1987, I experienced years of great learning, disasters and upheavals. For example, in 1985 my apartment and everything in it burned down and I was instantly homeless. Jack said the situation sounded like a *rite of passage* and that *some passages are so narrow you can't take anything with you.*

I took it as an opportunity to simplify my life so as to be undistracted from my primary intention to know God. I could not afford to find another apartment so I house-sat for friends and worked in exchange for room and board at several retreat centers in the area. Being cut instantly free from ordinary life and all belongings was disorienting, but at the same time made it seem easier to take on a renunciate life-style. As Bob Dylan put it, *When you got nothin', you got nothin' to lose.* After the initial shock, there was a definite feeling of freedom and that my life was moving in a new direction.

Pilgrimage

As life unfolded, I got a high-pressure job in a law firm in San Francisco. The environment was hectic and demanding. I feared I would never find the time and attention to draw closer to God in the life that I was living, but saw no other way at that time. Sometimes I would go entire days without remembering God at all, and when I came home I would be so tired that I would not meditate or spend any time in prayer.

Hoping to break this cycle I decided to carry a rosary with me all the time, keeping it in my pocket like a touchstone, something which, whenever my hand would touch it, would remind me to bring my attention back to the present moment and thereby to the only place God can be found.

At the beginning I was lucky if I followed through on that intention once or twice a day. Sometimes a week would pass and I would suddenly remember the rosary and have to search through my closet to find in which pocket I had left it. Then I would begin again. But little by little I began remembering it more often and finding crumbs of time in which to lift up my heart and remember the bigger picture.

Soon I actually found myself looking for and finding spare moments to spend like this, such as the numerous trips I took on the elevator. I kept this practice going for months, gradually increasing its frequency. Then, as often happens, God took me up on my small offering and the course of my life made a drastic turn, one that led to long periods of time to spend in prayer and meditation. Then, eventually, to a complete and total turnaround. Here's how it happened.

One day I saw a poster in a local bookstore advertising a talk being given by Bernadette Roberts at the now-defunct Melia Foundation in Berkeley. I reserved a place and went to hear her speak. I had no idea what to expect but I was very interested after reading her book.

I still had no interest in becoming a Christian; I thought of myself as following what I believed Jung had encouraged – examining my cultural religion with the intention of clearing the way to truly practicing

Buddhism. What I had read in Bernadette's books made me feel that what she had to say was something like a bridge between what I now understood and the deeper truths of the Christian path. Here, at the very least, was a Christian talking about consciousness.

The Foundation in Berkeley was an old house converted to a meeting place. During Bernadette's talk she spoke about the recent contact she had with the publishers of *The Laughing Man* magazine, which was put out by the Da Free John community.

She went on to talk about the writings of Da Free John and how he, like many others, had mistaken the end of ego for the end of self. The very fact that she was talking about my former guru was a shock. Though he had recommended her book to his community I had no idea she knew of him. It was very serendipitous. One of the rules of teacher-led, inward-facing spiritual communities such as the one surrounding Da Free John, is that you never criticize or even treat the teacher casually. Any problem that arises is never the teacher's fault – *you* are always the problem.

Hearing Bernadette Roberts point out the guru's shortcomings was empowering, and more important to me than her subject of 'no ego versus no self', which I only faintly if at all, understood. A few days later I wrote Bernadette a brief thank you note, telling her that I had just left the Da Free John community and that hearing what she had to say about him and his writings was a great help. She wrote back inviting me to attend a retreat she was giving in my area.

Sometime that same year, my father died. As he lay on what would be his death bed we talked about our life together, the good and the bad, in an open and honest way. He told me what it was like to be lying in the hospital bed knowing he would never get up again.

His only regrets were for the things he *didn't* do, rather than about anything he had done. We talked about our family problems but neither of us were in a blaming state of mind. We were just acknowledging life as it was then and now, at this important moment of his own passing. As I got up to leave the room he said, *Now Pat, whatever happens – you and I are…,* and he made a gesture, clasping his two hands together, meaning that we had finished what needed to be said. We were together now, and at peace with one another. That conversation was his last gift to me and it was a great and freeing one.

My father's death and our last conversation left me determined not to let life slip away without doing what was most important, to find and know God as much as is possible for me in this life.

I took two weeks bereavement time off work and went on a kind of self-imposed retreat, no phones, no TV or music, mostly just meditation, prayer, spiritual reading, walking and listening for God's voice within. I dedicated two hours every day to considering (envisioning) possible ways to live a life focused on God. At first I constantly got side-tracked into thinking about what I *did not* want, which was much easier than getting in touch with what I did want.

Initially I thought that I might want to become a nun. So I would picture myself: *Okay, here I am now, in my little cell. I know the schedule and this is what I'll be doing today and for the rest of my life – and I can forget everything else and just turn to God.* As soon as I pictured this clearly, I immediately knew that – no – this was not the right situation for me, not what I most deeply wanted.

I continued this exercise through many scenarios until it became clear – it was the same desire I had felt as a child when I wanted to join the nuns. I was looking for a situation and a place where I could open my heart and mind to the present moment to find God there, have a good, long time in silence and solitude and perhaps do some simple work like cleaning or cooking; tasks in which the mind and attention could be kept available for God. Though I still did not know how to bring this about, as soon as I got clear as to what I really wanted, a sense of peace descended.

The very next day after coming to this clarity, I received a letter from Bernadette, telling me that she had contacted Father Keating's community in New Jersey and made arrangements for me to work for my room and board if I wanted.

I wrote immediately to Fr. Keating and to Mary, the manager of the Contemplative Outreach Center, to tell them of my interest and ask about the possibility of a work-scholarship situation. I had doubts of course, wondering if I really needed to go anywhere, asking myself why I couldn't just do the same thing at home. Those were questions the mind had; the heart seemed to know better.

I had already met Fr. Keating and spent ten days on retreat with him at Snowmass, and because of that meeting, I now had an inkling of what it might mean to have a personal relationship with Christ, though I was still struggling with who or what Christ was or is. Probably the early years of being told stories about Jesus confused me – I could never imagine where Jesus the man could be right now in this moment and what possible difference a life lived (however perfectly) two-thousand years ago had to me or to anyone right now. Even if he was 'one with God' what did that have to do with my life now? Years of silent sitting had confirmed to me that this one present instant, what Meister Eckhart, Alan Watts and Bernadette Roberts call the *Now Moment*, is our key to the Truth. Where, except in a thought or a memory – was Jesus? These were questions I felt could be answered only in silence and solitude.

So, there I was, heading off to live in a Catholic retreat center. I could only hope that the reading I had done, the center's focus on meditation and having read the writings of Fr. Keating, Thomas Merton and Bernadette Roberts, would give me the background I needed to settle in there. Though I was in no way yet a Christian, the possibility of time alone with God was an irresistible urge. As I was preparing to go, my stepmother sent me a check from my father's estate – enough to pay off outstanding debts and arrange travel to Contemplative Outreach's Center in New Jersey, with a small amount of money left over.

My time of envisioning and coming to clarity had seemingly set off a string of opportunities and open doors, like tipping over the first in a long line of dominoes. Once again I gave away my belongings except what would fit in one suitcase, bought a train ticket, said good-bye to my (somewhat mystified) friends and headed out to find God.

When deciding to set out on this pilgrimage I

gave God a promise and an ultimatum – I would give myself to prayer and meditation – one-hundred percent – for the next year and if at the end of that year I had not truly found Him – knew He existed beyond any doubt – I would give up all this *spiritual stuff* and just *get married*, though I had no partner in mind. I wanted to know God existed as clearly and unequivocally as I knew that I have a body – no more lovely experiences that come and go, but an irrefutable, constant awareness of God.

Threatening to give up and *get married* was my way of saying that either I really find God and Truth, or I will stop meditating and seeking and just live an ordinary life. Regardless of the arrogance and naiveté of the request God answered my prayer beyond my wildest vision.

Grace Descends

I spent only a short time with Fr. Keating's community. It quickly became obvious that I needed more time in silent prayer than could be allowed given their busy community life and outreach program. After leaving, I spent a month house-sitting for a friend in upstate New York. Then I went to a Cistercian convent outside of Syracuse where I asked to work in exchange for room and board.

The sisters were wonderful and my stay there was unforgettable. After morning prayers my duties were to pick raspberries for the wine and jams they made to support the community, or to do housework. The afternoons were all mine for prayer, walking, and silence. One day while picking raspberries, my attention was drawn to a swarm of gnats. They danced around in a small circle, each one diving and swooping through the mass as if according to some design.

My eyes were suddenly open to the Oneness again and I *saw* the Intelligence that was dancing those tiny beings, what I now know to be the Logos, God that lives and is the world. When you get a glimpse of that bigger picture, and see yourself as dancing the dance along with everything else, you feel immediately free from all personal problems and concerns.

I wanted to stay there forever so I asked if I might be able to at least stay for the winter. They refused because I was not Catholic and they felt it would not be appropriate for me to stay so long. Nonetheless I loved my time there and I will never forget those sisters – or those little gnats!

Once again I was on the road with no idea of where to go next. I had promised God the entire year and it was not yet time to give up and go home, though everything I tried had not brought me to my goal. In desperation I called my old friend Jack Kornfield, and he offered to make arrangements for me to go to their Insight Meditation Society in Barre, Massachusetts, to join the three-month silent retreat that had just begun there.

I was unsure about the purely Buddhist environment. I felt I was settling for something, that a Buddhist retreat was not what I had wanted, but I was out of ideas. As it turned out the retreat in Barre was the perfect circumstance and the answer to my prayers. One month into my time there, something occurred which gave me the assurance, beyond doubt, that God exists and is more immediate than my own self, an instant that resulted in a permanent change of consciousness, of my very subjectivity. It is impossible to describe exactly *what* happened, because in a very real sense, *I* was not there when it happened. I will try to write about it as best I can.

The environment at the retreat was silence all day and night. We were instructed to consider ourselves to be completely alone, to the extent that even if you bumped into someone, no *sorry* or *excuse me* was necessary or wanted. No smiles across the dinner table were exchanged – in essence you were alone. Our practice was to stay present with whatever was arising to perception. We were not to write letters, read books or anything else, nor talk to anyone – just stay present with this present moment. The first week of the retreat was taken up with adjusting to hours of sitting and walking meditation. There was a lot of discomfort in the body and complaining in the mind.

After about ten days my arms and legs seemed to settle into the position and the pattern. Focusing what they called a *laser-beam of attention* to each moment felt very mental to me and hard to maintain. I found myself wanting to *feel* something, feel love for God and awe and gratitude and the positive feelings I associated with time on retreat. So in the afternoons, after lunch, I would go out into the woods and wander around. The place was surrounded by woods and boulders so this became my church, my prayer place. Here, instead of mentally gazing at what arose, I would lift my heart and soul to God and offer prayers of gratitude and petition. Refreshed, I would return willingly to walking-sitting, walking-sitting.

Though the meditation hours produced powerful insights, the times of prayer in the woods helped integrate them. After having to look constantly at the content of mind and perception, the movement away from self and toward God was a great relief.

I used my time in the woods to think about and try to answer some of my early childhood questions. Taking a walk in the woods one day I found myself once again thinking about existence and what life is and what awareness is. The next thought was: *I wonder what Bernadette Roberts would say about that.*

Like a stroke of lightning, the words came to mind, *Listen, when YOU die, it is not going to make two cents worth of difference what Bernadette knows. You better know it yourself!* This insight, I have never forgotten.

For several days, during meditation a change in my awareness would occur in which everything arising to consciousness would pass away immediately; the feeling was that all of life was rushing by, being formed, coming to awareness and then speeding to its end. Eventually my own sense of self became one more object racing by and for an instant, my *point of view* disappeared and I was swept along in the stream.

It was like nothing I had ever experienced and when I told the teacher who was assigned to interview me she seemed to recognize what I was describing, calling it *the state of arising and passing*. She said this was an important sign, but she did not say of what.

One evening a speaker encouraged us to push our limits, to try sitting longer or even through the night. I made a determination to stay up all night, meditating. Prior to that I kept to the prescribed hours of sitting and walking but on this night I set myself the task to stay with just the seated meditation, of being present to everything that arose moment to moment, thoughts, feelings, perceptions of any kind, to see if I could penetrate the arising phenomena and break through to the Emptiness beneath, to get a glimpse (hopefully) of a deeper Reality.

As I meditated late into the night, there came the sensation of expanding far beyond the usual limits of mind and body, awareness of an enveloping vastness where the "I" seemed like only a little blip. During this experience, I became aware that something was experiencing this vastness, aware of I as the *experiencer* of the vastness.

The very moment I caught *self* in the experience, *self* as a point of view dropped away. What had always been steadily the Background became All. My point of view (consciousness and the experiencer) was absorbed. There was no one having any experience. What remained is indescribable.

The closest I can come would be to use St Augustine's words, God was *closer to me than I am to myself.* God, like a vast ocean, and myself (thoughts, body, perceptions, emotions, point of view, the "I", and as far as I knew, *the entire sense of self*), disappeared.

As I was coming out of it, the sense of "I" was felt to be something like a small rainbow-colored oil spot floating on the vast surface of the ocean, a momentary, fragile, impermanent, insubstantial bit of something held together by the force of the ocean for a brief moment. The Ocean was the cause, ground and sustainer of the whole thing. In those timeless moments the center and circumference of self, had disappeared, absorbed in Something that had no center, no circumference.

It was a break in the stream of consciousness that had flowed on continuously since birth, a stream we do not even notice, until it stops. God is what IS and all I am is included in That. All movement of seeking God takes me from God, in God, I (and all) live forever – but not as me, not from my *point of view*.

This revelation of personal impermanence and the "*What*" that was permanent was life-changing and shook me to the core. I felt it also as an instant of tremendous relief, a relief from self. Imagine if, throughout your life, your consciousness was filled with a nonstop hum, a tone or sound so familiar and so much a part of your life that you are not aware of it.

Then one day, for a moment, the sound stops . . . then starts again. Now you recognize it, now you hear it always. Nothing I have written here comes close to expressing what occurred; those of you who have experienced it will recognize it. What happened was not deduced, imagined, realized or anything else.

Something Other was the cause and it wiped out even the experiencer for that moment. And after, I knew I had been irrevocably changed beyond the shadow of a doubt. As I had asked, now I knew – God IS. To spend my life dedicated to God was a valid choice – I could and indeed, must, give my life to that.

I can't say how long the whole thing lasted, but when I got up from my cushion and for days to follow, I could not describe the experience in words or even focus my mind on it. I could not reflect on it or *remember* it, because, you might say *I* had not been there when it happened; I had no *point of view* in it.

That something profound had happened, I knew, but when I tried to reflect on it the mind would immediately become empty and the heart would fill with a surge of love and peace. After a week or so I tried to talk to one of the teachers about it and he wisely encouraged me to just *put a question mark after it*, and go on.

The illusion that was dispelled with this experience is the previous notion that we, our feelings, energies, thoughts, personalities, etc., will somehow be transformed into the Divine. Now I knew that self is not, never was and can never be the Divine; that which is divine is something else entirely, not self.

It is not that *I am That* but rather *That is m*e. I knew I was changed as I had prayed to be changed, and forever. I wondered if I could possibly be at the end of the journey though I knew I was still too close to the experience to understand it fully.

Though it took place in a Buddhist retreat environment the experience at Barre was a confirmation of God's existence and closeness – which is not a Buddhist idea. When I returned from Barre I tried to explain it to Jack Kornfield. He told me I had now seen impermanence and experienced stream-entry.

However, my interest was not in my own impermanence, but on What remained when I was gone, the vast Ocean on which my little rainbow slick has (temporarily)formed. The difference between these two points of view may seem subtle, but it points directly at the difference between Christianity and Buddhism.

After the retreat in Barre, unsure what to do next, I stayed at my brother's house in Arkansas. They were away so I had time to be alone and integrate what had occurred. Everything had changed in a fundamental way though I was as yet unsure of exactly what was different. The molecules of my being seem to have been stretched or spread out so there was a sensation of being opened up, lighter and emptier.

There was a natural mindfulness, a sense of being present all the time, however the mind was empty of most reflective thought and the memory did not operate in the usual way. Thoughts and feelings had a superficial quality and did not in any way touch the silent center. Attention could be focused momentarily but could not be held on anything.

Unless spoken to in a way that required an answer the mind remained silent and at rest. I answered questions and took care of things with no premeditation or reflection.

I no longer felt the need to stay in the company of other practitioners or spiritual communities. I was free to go back home and just live ordinary life – in, with and for God. When my brother and his family returned I went back to California, prepared to just live my life.

The years I had spent studying and practicing Eastern religions had revolved around looking inward, self-knowledge and states of consciousness, but the experience at Barre was of God as totally Other, coming from *beyond* myself, including me but beyond me and not just another subjective, soon-to-fade experience. There was no way now to continue with meditation and other practices. Those practices were not capable of giving this Vision – when the tsunami comes, your swimming lessons are useless! God had fulfilled my request and nothing would ever be the same again.

After a month or so the various experiences began to fade. I could still sink into the silent center but thoughts began to have more strength to draw me out and involve me.

Even so I was aware that there was nothing I could do about these concerns except trust God. Emotions arose in response to situations but then dissipated on their own, like smoke out of an open window – with no discipline or self-control required on my part. There was also some form of altered vision that caused me to see God in everything or see everything as filled and lit with God. These experiences and insights were wonderful but I wondered why they were continuing. I had believed that these things are only given to those who don't have the faith to do without them.

I decided it might be shoring me up for what was down the road giving me the courage and strength to go through difficult times. And I was correct.

Though still not officially Catholic I started attended Mass at a nearby church. What I had learned at Barre was clearly about God and based on what I was reading at the time (Bernadette Roberts' *Path to No Self*), the path I was on was heading toward the Catholic Church. The only Catholic environments I was familiar with were those of convents and monasteries, so I was unpleasantly surprised by the lack of reverence in the churches where I attended Mass and the noisy socializing that went on before and right after. I made an effort to find chapels, hospitals and convents in my area, where the Mass was of a more contemplative nature.

I knew that the next step was to get past only being able to find God in silence, reverence and beauty – but I wasn't there yet. I was interested in what I had read and heard about the Eucharist and was considering the Church as the spiritual home I was seeking. What I understood and sensed was that the Eucharist was a silent, always available, point of contact with God.

Heading Home

There was a giant obstacle standing in the way of my joining the Catholic Church, and that was Jesus. I was still hung up on my childhood ideas about the man and didn't have another way to think about him. What did Jesus Christ have to do with my life here and now?

I could not see how one *incarnation* (as I thought of it then) was greater than another – wasn't the Buddha kind of a Christ also? If so, other than being an inspiration, I felt that I had no use or need for Jesus.

To be fair, I could at least vaguely grasp the Christ, the Word (Form) out of which the world and each instant is formed, but the man Jesus? I just couldn't grasp it, and since Jesus seemed to be at the very center of the Catholic faith, how to get past him and into the Church was the unanswered question. It wasn't enough that I trusted what others said about it; if I couldn't get it myself I wasn't willing to make the commitment. I knew for sure that God was most certainly with me, without my ever having had to think twice about Christ.

Around that time, I read an essay by Bernadette Roberts, entitled *How Christ is Different from Us, or One of a Kind Among Men?*[5]. This was very much my own question so I was eager to hear what she had to say about it:

> "Intellect alone cannot prove the existence of God or the Absolute, and neither can it prove the divinity of Christ. For most people, however, the intuition of an ultimate Absolute is not a problem, while belief that Christ IS the Absolute is not such an easy intuition, and for some it is a problem. Belief that Christ was a holy man who attained mystical awareness of oneness with the Absolute is not a problem, but then it is also not the truth of Christ. The question Christ poses is how the one eternal Absolute could possibly incarnate itself as a single human being. The question of whether or not it has happened is secondary to its very possibility. Although the problem of God is equally the problem of Christ, yet Christ extends the problem by raising the question of what the Absolute can or cannot do. That the Absolute can incarnate Itself confronts us with a step-in belief that may never satisfy the intellect or lend itself to simple intuition. But this possibility is the mystery of Christ, a mystery that not only boggles the mind, but may even bother it."

---

[5] *What is Self?*, 93.

To grasp the idea that God could be in some way personal, it is necessary to first realize we are *personal* and what that means. As a Westerner trying for many years to practice Buddhism, what I thought I was doing was attempting to not assume the personal self. In my heart, what I was really doing was trying to find God.[6] The Buddha did not deny God. Coming as he did from a Hindu life and culture, such a thought would not even arise.

What I had learned was that the Buddha told his monks that such questions were not of much use. He said that one who tries to understand Ultimate Truth is like someone shot with a poisoned arrow who refuses to take it out or have it taken out before finding out what kind of poison was used, who shot the arrow,

---

[6] There is a story circulating that the abbot of an American Zen Training Center once burst into a room of Zen meditators, walked to the front of the room, and said, "You people are all looking for God. That is **not** Buddhist!", and then stomped out. I heard Bernadette tell this story, but I also heard it from someone who was there.

where were they from, etc. What Buddha taught was the truth of *suffering, and the end of suffering*.

Buddhist thought, as I understood it, taught that there was a mysterious silent, immovable but dynamic Emptiness, out of which all manifestation arose like bubbles in a boiling soup. We bubble up out of that boiling sea, have our time of existence – which may include many lifetimes – then fall back and are reabsorbed into it – never truly separate from it.

Individual characteristics and destiny was based on past lives and all life is an illusion, though the pain seems real enough. Now how do you get a Christ out that? What could such a thing be – a bigger or more special bubble? All one can make of it is that one of the bubbles realized its true nature, its Buddha Nature, and after teaching us what he knew, was reabsorbed like all else. To think that God could or would do this, simultaneously does away with our inherent divine nature; if we are all bubbling up, how are we not all Christs?

In *What is Self?,* I read for the first time the idea of the Unmanifest Divine. This fit very well with my

Western Buddhist idea of the Void so I could grasp it enough to accept it.

To think about the Logos, the second person of the Trinity, as *all that is manifest of the Unmanifest*, was an important step. Then to think of Christ as the union of manifest divine nature (Logos) and human nature, the ultimate destiny of everyone, lifted me out of the anthropomorphic and limited ideas of Christ with which I was struggling.

These new (to me) ideas reminded me of: *Form is Emptiness/Emptiness is Form; Form is not different from Emptiness; Emptiness is not different from Form* – part of the Buddhist Heart Sutra which is chanted every day in Zen Centers around the world. In considering these ideas, I was beginning to see the difference between Jesus and Christ. I was beginning to see how Christ could be the Now Moment.

Of course, even this beginning of an answer brought up more questions, for example: what about the Incarnation, which (like most people) I thought of as Jesus' birth two-thousand years ago? Form (the

Manifest Divine) obviously existed before that. It would take years and much help to come to peace with those mysteries and I was really only able to do that through prayer and further study, and consideration of books like *The Real Christ* by Bernadette Roberts. But at least now I was finding an openness to, and an opening into, Christianity.

What had been revealed at Barre took away the attachment to a spiritual identity, to only be with and be known by other spiritual seekers, and especially the need to stay close to the socially accepted Buddhists that I knew. All the trappings and glamor of being involved in Eastern practices became an anathema to me – I had been born into an ostensibly Christian country so why try to be something else? What God had shown me was not Its preference for any one religion, path or technique – but Its oneness with all. So why not blend into the surroundings, forget myself and live *"hidden in Christ"* (Colossians 3:3).

The ancient contemplative tradition of the Catholic Church produced true saints like Mother

Teresa of Calcutta and masters of wisdom such as John of the Cross, Meister Eckhart, not to mention the modern ones I had the good fortune to read and even meet in my own life, such as Bernadette Roberts, Father Keating, Sister Ruth Burrows.

Its religious orders honored silence and solitude which were so close to my own heart, and produced writings about contemplative prayer, a kind of deep prayer, that was far more than mere words spoken in God's direction. So I was ready to join the Church, not because I understood all its mysteries or believed all its dogma but because of the Eucharist, which I believed to be the silent, ever present access to God in the immediate Christ.

Coming Home

You have not chosen me: but I have chosen you...
~John 15:16

I went to the nearest Catholic Church and spoke with the priest about becoming a Catholic. It was early in the year and the RCIA two-year course required to join the Church was already nearly complete. So the priest sent me instead to a retreat center at a Dominican College and put me under the tutelage of Sister Suzanna Malarkey (her real name).

She gave me a copy of the Dutch Catechism and we agreed to meet weekly for the next 6 weeks. I began reading with some trepidation, sure I was going to get stuck and stopped on some too-conservative idea but with her guidance I was able to ask the right questions and get helpful answers.

At the end of the six weeks, the priest came to the retreat center and with some Dominican sisters and a friend of mine as witnesses, I joined the Catholic Church. At the ceremony of confirmation (I had already been baptized) when the priest put the oil on my forehead and the white shawl around my shoulders a vision took form.

Looking down a long tunnel I saw priests, monks and nuns lined up on either side, all looking at me. St. John of the Cross was one of them. I felt I had joined the lineage, as they would say in Buddhism, entering something ancient, hidden and vast. Home at last.

After the ceremony the priest said to me that at the moment of placing the shawl around my neck he felt something special happen and asked me if I felt it too. I had felt it and was happy to get his confirmation. Now, after more than thirty years in the Church, I am aware of how unusual this confirmation service is; that priests do not make 'house calls' to bring people into the Church, and usually people do not take one-on-one instructions with a nun at a retreat center.

I saw Sister Malarkey many years later and she asked me if I was *still a Catholic*. When I answered yes enthusiastically – she smiled and said, *I guess it took after all*.

As it says in the Buddhist Heart Sutra, *A glimpse of the Absolute is not yet enlightenment*. I had been given the glimpse, but was still in the process of being transformed. I had doubts that someone like myself would have been granted the grace to know God. You certainly couldn't see it by looking at me. I thought I needed some outside confirmation of what had occurred.

I complained about this so often that Jack Kornfield. finally wrote out a parchment manuscript confirming what he called *my realization* authorizing me to teach or direct others. I still have the manuscript, though receiving it didn't help. Only God can affirm and confirm Itself to us.

No one else in the world can do this for God, so even when someone you respect and trust tells you that you are one with God, it doesn't penetrate the doubt. Either you think they don't know you well enough or they don't know the state well enough.

On the other hand, when you meet or hear the words of someone who has had your same experience you recognize it immediately. The Holy Spirit illuminates and affirms the communication and you recognize it. You would not say to the person, *You must be in the Unitive State,* but you both know, you recognize each other.

Except for these rare occasions, you may and most likely will, spend the rest of your life unrecognized by anyone – except God. And that is as it should be. This is the true meaning of being *hidden in Christ.* Having been a doubting person all my life, I now came to see the value of doubt. Not knowing meant I had to trust God for everything. The desire for absolute certitude is a demand of the self. In moving ahead without that certitude, we develop trust and faith and see the outline of That which lives the world.

The state of things at this point: Going to Mass often but, due to old friendships and connections, still attending Buddhist meditation sessions; trying to live hidden in Christ in the world but hiding Christ from the Buddhists.

Still translating Buddha Nature or Void to Absolute or God, and still wondering about Jesus (though not about Christ any longer). Though I was told that Buddhists did not believe in God, I translated that in my mind to the idea that Buddhists were just giving God another name. I told myself it was because Buddhism had practices that were useful, something that Christianity did not offer. I could not understand *love is the way, the practice,* because I still thought of love as a feeling, a feeling I only occasionally *felt* for God and never for Jesus.

Though I thought I was free of it, I was obviously still clinging to my identity as a Buddhist and hiding being Catholic – making myself what I called a *closet Catholic*. The fence-sitting was becoming obvious, though I didn't yet want to admit it.

Many of my old Buddhist friends had bad experiences with the Church, many called themselves recovering Catholics. I was too cowardly at that time to admit to them that I had now joined the very Church that they considered to be at least hypocritical and disappointing, and at worst, a complete and utter scandal.

While my outer life was stuck there, my inner life continued to deepen and grow. My desire to sink-in, and the need to be alone to do this frequently conflicted with the demands of my job. I had been hired to administer the Buddhist Spirit Rock Center, which required constant telephone conversations, meetings, writing, bookkeeping, staffing and other administrative duties.

When I accepted the job I made a two-year commitment but shortly thereafter I began to wonder if I would be able to continue for that long. I was aware that I was not doing as good a job as I had been capable of in the past, due to continuing spiritual experiences which now came even when not sitting in meditation. Periods of absorption made it hard to concentrate and attend to the complications of running a large organization.

I looked into various monasteries and Catholic communities, but none seemed right. I just had to continue with things as they were and trust God for the rest.

While working for Spirit Rock, I spoke with a visiting Hinayana monk. When I described my present state of awareness he asked me what I was *doing* relative to the still center. I told him I was trying to remain passive to it, and he said, *That's too active. Trying* to remain passive is not really passive. He told me that I shouldn't go on long meditation retreats any more, that the silent center would now teach me everything I need to know; learn to trust it. He said if I still felt I needed to practice he would give me a mantra. *Here*, he said, *is the only mantra you will ever need*: **This** *is the way it is.*

Darkness

In early March of 1989, I went on retreat at New Camaldolese in Big Sur with Bernadette Roberts and a group of others. Sitting in the Chapel after Mass one day I saw the room fill with a great light which seemed to be centered around the candle on the altar.

The light entered body and mind with each breath. Walking out of the chapel Bernadette turned to me and asked, *What happened in there*? I took her aside and began telling her about the experience. After a few minutes she turned from me, waved to the rest of our group and told them, *Hey, come over here and hear what happened to Pat!*

I was very surprised! In the Buddhist culture, you might share an experience with a teacher – but you certainly don't talk about these kinds of experiences with others. I managed to stammer out a description of what happened and then later I told Bernadette that it had surprised me that she would have me tell everyone about the experience.

She looked askance at me and said, *Did you think that experience was just for you?* Another example of new understanding for me as a Christian.

Although now a *bona fide* Catholic, in my heart I wondered why I was still clinging to the fence, attending Mass and Christian retreats but unable to fully give up involvement with Buddhist practices and friends. I was further confused by hearing about Catholic monks and nuns who studied and practiced Buddhism. I had even been to a Zen Center in a Catholic Church! Out of this confusion, when I was offered the chance to move to the Sonoma Mountain Zen Center, I took it.

Living there and practicing Zen exacerbated my indecision. I was in a constant inner (and sometimes outer) argument with the practices and principles of Zen. I was going to Mass as often as possible, and though I knew it was time to be honest about it, I was reluctant to give up my old ways.

As shallow as I knew it was, I was still attached to being with those who were doing the really interesting thing – Buddhism – whereas Catholicism was definitely not cool! Fortunately, the Eucharist was doing its transforming work in me, and beyond my conscious awareness I was being changed.

Looking back at it, I think I went to live at the Zen Center so I could more easily give in to spiritual experiences and periods of ecstasy. I sometimes had the idea that the spiritual journey was nearly over and that there must only a ragged shred of self remaining.

It had not yet occurred to me that my attachment to blissful or even empty states and experiences might be something to take a look at. I finally became suspect when I saw that I was refusing to live the daily schedule at the Zen Center; I didn't want to work or do anything that would draw me out of the inner silence and peace.

I sometimes sat through the night absorbed. I would have to leave that absorption when others disturbed me or demanded my attention. Eventually the disturbance and the aggravation it caused clued me in to the fact that the self was still fully present and in charge, and that the experiences were not God.

So I forced myself to return to the daily schedule, to work, go to meals and engage in conversation with others. It was hard to do, like being madly in love and then agreeing not to see the beloved person. I wanted to go all the way with God, whatever that would take and remembering all that I had read about the need to move beyond experience, it was clear that something further was required.

Surprisingly the Christian mysteries began to spontaneously explain themselves to me – while in meditation in the Zendo. As I would stand up from my zafu a thought about the Trinity would arise or about the Logos as Form, or about the meaning of the Cross. Perhaps this is what is meant by being pursued by the hound of heaven. Christ was drawing me like a magnet.

I was learning that the Christian contemplative does not have to trust in her ability to take each instant apart and find God there between the molecules. Perhaps it would be possible to train ourselves to be able to do that. But the true way is to take the focus off self and self's experiences; whatever self does or puts together is undone in the end. We are left with only one resort – God. The necessity to understand and accept the limits of efforts, and accept our helplessness and dependence on God makes the Christian way an anathema to the wise. The Cross is its icon. As Pierre-Marie Dumont beautifully puts it:

> "This icon invites us to meditate on the unfathomable mystery of our God, who gives the greatest proof of his omnipotence in his kenosis, his 'emptying out' of himself, his renunciation of power in any form, for the benefit of each and every one of us."

Regardless of the problems of living at the Zen Center, monastic life has a particular beauty. I think anyone who has lived it for a while would agree. I loved the quiet beauty of the mornings at the Zen center. Mist rising into the redwoods and falling back down as rain on redwoods and rooftops.

The crunch of gravel underfoot as, in the darkness, black robed figures silently stride up the hill to the Zendo, following the deep sound of the bell. The companionable silence of shoe removal in the outer room, bare feet on cold wood floor, the daily rhythm.

Four in the morning is manageable when no one speaks, it becomes an extension of sleep and dream. Incense, candlelight, your place marked out, one black square and circle. Bow, ease down, robe settled, assume form and silence as others softly rustle in and take their places, all seated, quietly waiting.

Only the sound of the rain on the roof, as Roshi enters, the soft shuffle of his feet on the mats, the hiss of a match as he lights his incense before the picture of his teacher. Then the shared silence. Then chanting. Slowly waking up.

Beautiful though it was, I was coming to the understanding that it is not possible to meditate one's way to God or bring about a final and complete surrender into the Background. Only That which created us and is greater than us can fully transform us.

No matter how quiet and empty mind could be, self is not undone but always returns to take charge. One evening during walking meditation, a strange sensation arose, as if I were a candle flame about to be snuffed out. Apprehension and a sense of something powerful and beyond my control came over me. At the first opportunity I ran out of the Zendo and over to the main house. I wanted to be around others, noise, activity – anything rather than just to hold still and let this snuffing take place. Control was being severed, but I did not know what was happening.

Negative emotions and thoughts came pouring out, as if a plug had been pulled somewhere in my being and every problem, doubt and difficulty I ever had come flowing past and out. It felt like opening Pandora's box. In desperation I called Jack Kornfield – I had to talk to someone.

He encouraged me to remember compassion, suggesting the Buddhist female form of Kuan Yin, compassion personified – in other words find some way to remember love. But I could not do it except for maybe thirty seconds. Something beyond my control was happening and I didn't know if it was good or bad.

That night marked the beginning of a hellish year. For a time, I continued to live at the Zen Center, but I began feeling sick, physically and emotionally. There was an abiding feeling of heaviness and dread no matter what I did, and no peace or satisfaction in anything.

Sitting in meditation was torture and I argued constantly with Roshi about having to attend every session. I thought perhaps I was experiencing something hormonal or physical or maybe chronic depression and I wrote to a wise friend describing what was happening, asking if she thought it could be depression.

She assured me in no uncertain terms that it was no such thing, and encouraged me to endure it for the love of God. She questioned why I thought I had to know what was causing it. Now was the time to just trust God – and maybe read how it went with the saints.

It was good advice, though my love of God was without loving feelings of any kind because I was now incapable of them. Faith had been deepening for years now, and I was as aware of God as I was of myself. I wondered if this was another Dark Night. My confusion at the time was exacerbated by trying to know where I was on the path, when truly it didn't matter at all and only God really knew anyway.

I remembered Da Free John writing: *Our destiny is uncertain but our obligation is clear*. When I talked to Roshi about it, he encouraged me to study the koan: *When you have climbed to the top of a one-hundred-foot pole, how do you go forward?* The answer of course is that you have to jump off – leave the security of the heights and go back to the basics, into unknowing.

As quickly as I could arrange it I packed up and left the Zen Center. I wanted to stop meditating and I no longer felt or wanted any inspiration from Zen. I left for Kansas and my family. On the way I made a stop in Amarillo, Texas to be a volunteer cook at a teacher training led by Father Keating. I had done plenty of retreat cooking at the Zen Center and since I was hoping to involve myself in more Catholic activities, this seemed like a good entry.

As I walked into the Benedictine monastery where the teacher training was to be held, a very familiar smell caught my attention – Japanese incense! Following my nose I came to a door and peeking in, saw a large room all set up for Zen sitting! There was even someone in a black Zen robe lighting the incense. As I was to discover this is not the only Catholic monastery or retreat center where Zen sitting has made inroads.

At the time I was encouraged by seeing Catholics practicing Zen as I thought perhaps I too would also be able to somehow combine the two traditions. I finished my week-long job as cook and continued on to Kansas.

Once I arrived I quickly found a job as a cook at a Catholic retreat center and a shabby but acceptable place to live. What had begun that night at the Zen Center intensified. I developed mysterious hives (doctors could not explain it) all over my body and began experiencing the effects of newly diagnosed diabetes. But the most significant changes took place in my inner life and subjectivity. Awareness was stuck in the present moment. Having heard that one way to enlightenment was to *Be Here Now*, one might think the state of always being present would be a lovely one.

However, this was the equivalent of seeing empty phenomenon continuously arising with no God, without meaning, without feeling.

That description does not in any way express the painful reality. When the mind, memory and emotions do not provide background or explanations for what is perceived, phenomena just arise to the senses and seems empty. Mind and body both felt heavy and dead. I could not use my memory or imagination. If I wanted to remember anything I would have to stop whatever else I was doing and concentrate, following a line of events back to the event I wanted to recall. Memory would not bring up anything on its own. Because of this, the thinking mind was still, but it was not a peaceful stillness.

It was a dead feeling and yet full of struggle, as if each thought had to be dredged up out of mud and held in place by some kind of force or else fall back into nothingness immediately. I could not use my imagination or think about the future, at least not for more than about fifteen minutes ahead.

For example, when I awoke in the morning I would think – now I'll go to the bathroom and brush my teeth. If I tried to think about what to wear or what might be happening later that day I would be unable to do so. In fact, trying to do this caused me so much pressure in the head that I stopped trying.

After brushing my teeth, I could dimly consider getting dressed and then think about going into the kitchen and eating breakfast, and on and on, inching forward through time as if in a dense fog that only allowed seeing one-foot head.

If mentally looking forward or backward in time was impossible it was even worse trying to look inward. My feeling self was filled with anguish and discomfort but for no apparent reason. Everything, every activity, even thinking or remembering or just sitting in a chair, carried with it a sense of having to fight a great fight but with no strength at all. I felt weak and at the same time driven somehow to keep going. All around me I saw meaningless phenomena, void of all meaning, seemingly without God.

I would like to say that even so I knew God was there – but truthfully, I felt unable to *know* anything. Looking back now I can relate it to what John of the Cross wrote about *walking in darkness, but secure,* but the *security* did not come from the mind or even the feeling.

Form and emptiness were *one thing*, true, but a dead thing. Somehow, I never doubted God was there, though how I can say I knew this I don't know. I believed there was something wrong with me, some lack or weakness, but I did not really know how or what I could do about it.

It was the most difficult time of my life and I constantly felt I was not up to it. I remember sitting in my car one day after struggling through eight hours of work, dull, dead, and with no idea what was wrong with me, wondering if I could ever commit suicide – anything to stop the pain. I thought I was possibly going mad.

The only thing that kept me from checking into the hospital and confessing to some kind of a psychotic episode was that I could see that on a practical level I was not behaving like a crazy person. I was cleaning my house, taking baths, paying my bills, going to work – I was taking care of myself.

The people outside of me did not respond to me as someone acting strangely; apparently to the outside world I appeared the same as always. I had no one near me with whom to talk about this and that, I believe, was to the good.

No one can really get hold of your inner state and they can only compare it to their own, or to what they have read. So even if you can talk about things like this with a friend you end up feeling they don't really get it or that you didn't explain it properly.

Then occurred the only thing in my life thus far that I would call a true miracle. After a month of barely holding it together, I was awakened at 4:00 AM one morning by a phone call telling me that I had to come in to work unexpectedly that day. It felt like the last straw.

I couldn't take it. I was totally overwhelmed. I couldn't even cry. I paced back and forth for a while, literally groaning. Then I sat down and grasped my hands into a posture of prayer, something I almost never did. I prayed, not to Kuan Yin as Jack had suggested, but to Mary, the Mother of Jesus who Catholics said could intercede for us.

I prayed with all my heart, *Mary, I don't believe in you. I don't even know what or where you could possibly be. But if you are anything, please, please help me, because I cannot keep going like this!*

In the blink of an eye the whole tortured state of being began to drain out of me, like water going out of a bathtub. I felt it go, out of my head, down and out of my body. For the next hour I sat there in a state of calmness and peaceful joy, completely restored. I felt God's presence strongly and also a loving presence that I now know was Mary. I was given to know that this present period of difficulty was God's purifying work, that periods of pain and emptiness are part of the path and no matter how dark things are, God is ever present.

I remembered then, the commitment I had made to trust all to God and felt gratitude in seeing that my offer had been accepted. After an hour of this rest I was able to acknowledge that, with God's help, I could take it and if it was part of God's plan for me, I wanted it.

The very moment I acknowledged that to myself, unbelievably it all came right back – rising from below as if the bathtub was filling with the same dirty water again. Everything was exactly as before, exactly as painful and terrible, not a bit different or less, but the knowledge that this was somehow God's mercy (through the prayers of Mary) made all the difference. I knew I could take it, that I wanted to live through it, no matter what. Though I did not feel any less pain than before there was now this tiny space of distance from it, right there in the midst of it.

This was what the Church means when it talks about *Mary's Yes*, I could now hold still in God's hands. I still had no idea *what* or *where* Mary could possibly be, but I never again doubted that she, like God, IS, and is always there to help us, if we ask.

Fence-Sitting

After only four months in Kansas I ran back to California, thinking maybe being near friends and familiar sights would make things easier. I knew I would miss certain people in Kansas, my son and his wife for sure, and also his father, my former husband who is still like family.

I was born and raised in the prairie and I know it has a beauty all its own, but California is my home, and I wanted to go home. As I boarded the train the only goal I could set for myself on this trip was to try not to hyperventilate in front of people!

That is how fragile I was. I wasn't at all sure that I could do it. I was still covered with hives, weak and shaky and unable to think or remember at all.

In California it was made evident that God would take care of me in every way and my responsibility was to trust in and rely on that. I was powerless to do the things that were necessary to live – get a job, find a car and a place to live.

In my condition I had no idea how I could possibly do any of those things and yet I was completely broke and had to support myself. Many of the same difficult symptoms remained but there was one important change.

It was like having two sets of eyes: one set was looking out on the world before me and seeing it, though the vision was not clear or strong. The other set of eyes were held inwardly gazing into a vast field that was empty of thought or feeling but intensely alive. These inner eyes were fixed open and staring, there was no rest for them and nothing at all to see. Ninety percent of my attention was held in the inner vision. No work or activity could bring me out of it and at the same time I could not purposefully turn to it or look inwardly at it.

Miraculously in two weeks I had a home, a job, a car, and all without feeling that I had made any effort at all. I remember getting dressed for an interview for the job for which I was eventually hired, and thinking to myself that there was no way I would be able to convince anyone to hire me.

I couldn't even consciously remember how to work in an office much less present my talents and skills in a saleable fashion. I walked into the interview in a completely blank state and walked out with a job. It was amazing. What this verified was that I had to have complete faith in God now because I could do nothing on my own. It was faith unaccompanied by emotions or feelings of fervor; I just had to assume it.

All the ways that I knew previously to pull myself up and redirect my life were not available – even in the face of great need. Living this way is like having your hands tied behind your back and having to run down a very steep hill – at any moment one wrong step and you will be on your face. Yet there was no choice, the hill itself rushes you forward.

I have told this rather long story to express how far from bliss and peace the spiritual journey can take you, and yet even at the furthest point of pain and darkness, God is right there beside you. What I went through and what I learned helped me drop false expectations of peace and bliss, and most importantly in my case, to stop putting trust in *feelings*, trusting instead in what is silent and unmoving beyond feelings.

Though I cannot pinpoint a definitive end to these hard times, after a month or two in California I had at least learned to function in this strange state. That was good enough, and I was grateful for it. All that was necessary was provided.

A permanent change in my subjectivity had taken place. Life and awareness centered on the living Emptiness, the same spot of Emptiness that had revealed itself so clearly both at Barre and in meeting Mary in Kansas. It can be described as emptiness only because something is there that cannot be perceived the way we usually perceive things. In time, ordinary consciousness became centered on it and awareness of the Emptiness becomes less spectacular and more ordinary, it's just the way things are.

When I thought about those months in Kansas and then continuing in California, I admit I persisted in trying to figure out where I was on the path. But while there are certain patterns in the path to God, it is a totally individual thing – which might be another sense in which God could be said to be personal.

There is just a lot we don't know as we go along, and we don't need to know. To follow the path as far as we can during our life means to hand over control and eventually hand over even our understanding and knowing, as well as whatever we learned from others. As the Hindu sage, Nisargadatta once said, *Understanding is extra*. That is a profound truth, and a difficult one for self to accept. Self wants to *know*, but it doesn't happen that way. One thing this period of difficulty taught me is that it is not so much a matter of handing anything over; it is more about surviving when God takes something away.

My preference for the gypsy life was fast fading, and I was coming to feel that there might be advantages to staying in one place. Though I still had to endure occasional difficulties, there were moments of peace and joy – always unreasonable – and times of deep absorption in God. The difficulties were mostly physical: hives continued and there was an episode which the doctor said was a heart attack. Strange pains and symptoms appeared and disappeared.

The onslaught was exhausting. But right there beside it was the awareness of a silent, unmoving Presence, and that had a calming effect, even in the midst of whatever happened. Life continued, I continued, though changed. One example of the change was that I experienced what is sometimes referred to as a witnessing experience, wherein life and awareness of self arise as always but simultaneously with an awareness of the unmoving Ground, sort of like being the movie screen as well as the movie.

Whatever interior problems I experienced were due to the habit of putting my attention on and participating in the affairs and problems of my life, and not on that silent Presence. I wasted a lot of time sorting through the over-flowing drawers of my mind, when I would have been much better served to drop the self-concern and turn to God.

The key to the present movement is to remain passive to interior silence, to trust it as we trust God Itself, and to let nothing take it from us. While the center acts as a magnet, drawing everything into itself, in order to be wholly drawn in, we must first abandon all that is contrary to silence – all the disturbing movements of mind and emotions.

We gradually abandon these by remaining passive to the center on one side, and to the movements on the other – that is, we let the movements pass, not getting mentally involved. Bernadette says it like this:

> "Our part is to remain passive to the inner silence and trust it. This trust is so imperative at this time that I would say the speed with which unification is completed is proportional to the degree of passivity."[7]

It would have been easier to go through this period while living the life of a religious. In that circumstance, one would have the daily schedule of prayer and meditation, as well as mature contemplatives to talk with.

As it was, I had to figure things out for myself. I tried to return to meditating but couldn't focus the attention. The awareness of the Ground was like a great

---

[7] *Path to No Self*, 52.

black field behind or beneath ordinary consciousness, there all the time, unmoved and unmovable, and then sometimes bearing down on the mind so strongly that everything else was obliterated. That sounds good, however there was no satisfaction for self in it.

The reader may be shocked to hear that I was still participating in Buddhist meditation and retreats. In my heart, I was Catholic – but I stubbornly refused to admit it to others and honor it as my true and only spiritual home.

When I thought about the Church and all its well-known errors, I did not want to be identified with it. I allowed media content to advise my thinking. Exclusivity of access to the Eucharist, birth control, abortion, homosexual marriage – everything the Church stood for went against everything popular American culture defended. The priest abuse scandals were everywhere in the news. All the while, Buddhism appeared to be (certainly in the media) about peace and compassion, meditation and psychological health. I was still avoiding what Christians call the scandal of the Cross.

Still, I loved the Mass and was strengthened and encouraged by every contact with the Eucharist. One day at Mass they read the story of the *pearl of great price* (Matt. 13:45-46). It struck me that, though the man found the pearl in the middle of the field, he couldn't just take it out and keep it.

He reburied it and then went to buy the whole field. How was I going to *buy the entire field?* How to accept and acknowledge the Church as God's vehicle on earth? And yet it seemed to me that to turn away from all the Church teaches, while still receiving the Sacrament was a kind of stealing.

Soon however, the inner conflict was to be resolved, and forever, by a revelation of the deeper truth of the Blessed Sacrament, which changed everything and sealed me to Christ forever.

Regardless, and with no defensible excuse, I returned again to living at the Zen Center. Immediately, however, I began questioning myself: was there any use in sitting hour after hour in the Zendo, tired and in pain?

Was I just creating a distraction and a protection for myself by holding on to both practices? By not making a commitment to one or the other I did not allow either tradition to make its full demand on me. I remained in charge of where this little ship was sailing.

I convinced myself I moved back to the Center because I enjoyed living in the woods close to nature, and enjoyed having others to share dinner and a laugh with once in a while. I was very comfortable with the monastic schedule.

In an effort to hang on, I had even taken Zen lay ordination, though I think both the Roshi and I had grave misgivings about it. I also had an ulterior motive – I was beginning to think about getting older and I believed that, without retirement money or prospects, I could do a lot worse than ending up in such a situation.

I had not yet recognized a life-long tendency of mine: to find and connect with an organization to tell me what to believe and how to go (first with Free John, then with Zen, and finally even with the Church).

After taking on all the practices and following all the directions (though not always in agreement with or believing in them), the point would come in which I would feel I had lost my own direction and have to separate myself. At this time, however, I knew God was in charge and could boot me out of there at a moment's notice. If so, so be it. And that is what happened.

The day came when I finally admitted to the Roshi that I could no longer do the long meditation sittings. I told him I wanted to live there without doing the many sessions of meditation and instead, work longer hours than those doing Zen training. He was naturally hesitant to change the practice in any way that might dilute it for others, but he said he would think about it. I had finally been true to and admitted my own inner truth.

In the end, Roshi decided he did not want to make such an exception, and so I left. Once again, no money, no job. Once again, living by faith – and what was beginning to look like foolishness. I wondered if I would just drift around forever and if that was really God's will for me. I knew it would mean sacrifices –

living by faith doesn't mean being patient until you get everything that you want.

It means accepting everything that you get including problems, hardships, pain and difficulty, welcoming, as Rumi wrote, *every visitor* (sadness, sickness, etc.) *as a messenger from beyond.*

Miraculously, I was once again able to get a place to live and a good job. Near my work, there was a beautiful old Church where I could attend Mass every day on my lunch hour.

At last I was ready, willing and able to be honest about my Christianity. No more hiding. I had finally gotten off the fence and even burned it. The habitual focus on inner conflict and outer problems was fading away. In any case I was no longer paying much attention to it; it had become unimportant. The demands of ordinary life kept me busy enough. That state of things was as good as enlightenment as far as I was concerned!

In my new little apartment, I had more solitude and silence than when I lived at the Zen Center. Though I had a few friends in town I was mostly alone and on my own. Without the demands of the spiritual search to keep me busy a new thing appeared in my life – spare time. It would have been easy to fill up that time with distractions but nothing interested me, to such a degree that, sometimes, I questioned why I continued to live.

I knew I was at a turning point and I began to wonder what God might have in mind for my life. Of course it was a waste of time to ask this question because there was nothing I could do to know or help God accomplish His purposes anyway. My practice was doing whatever was next, waiting on God and spending time in prayer. I was at peace. Things had reached a point where God was about to put the final piece to the puzzle.

While attending daily Mass during my lunch hour I began having an unusual, and ultimately life-changing experience. Every day as I walked into the Church I was immediately overcome by a blissful feeling – a kind of languor, on the edge of full ecstasy.

Moving to the pew to sit down was like walking through honey, I had to push against the weight of it – but it was a delightful feeling. The experience continued throughout the service until I walked up the aisle and received Communion. As soon as I consumed the Host, the blissful feeling disappeared immediately and completely. The disappearance was sudden and startling and therefore very noticeable, like music that suddenly stops. I walked back to my seat and was just myself, no bliss, no swoon, nothing, just ordinary consciousness. The difference between the two states was undeniable.

The odd thing was that the experience seemed backward. You would think that blissful feeling would *begin* with consuming the Host, but no, the powerful joyful feeling *ended* immediately upon reception of Communion. I had never heard of such a thing and no one I asked about it had heard of it either.

And the fact that this happened every day without fail made me suspect I was being shown something – though I was mystified as to what it might be. Later that year I attended a retreat with Bernadette Roberts and I described the experience to the group, of the strange juxtaposition of bliss as soon as I walked in the door followed by receiving Communion and the sudden end of the bliss.

I told them that this experience had continued for an entire year. Even Bernadette said she had never heard of such a thing, that for most people it was exactly the opposite. I left as mystified as before and the experience continued.

A year passed and in 1998, at another retreat with Bernadette and a different group of participants, I again described my experience – which now had gone on for nearly two years. Bernadette expressed surprise that it was still happening. Then she stopped talking and seemed to be thinking, while the rest of the group jumped in with all kinds of advice and possible explanations. As I recall it, Bernadette sat with her eyes closed, as if thinking. Then she suddenly clapped her hands and said, *I've got it*! She said that God was trying to show me that *no-experience* is closer to the truth than bliss. Upon hearing that, I immediately understood.

God was indeed using this experience to show me the truth of Its non-experiential nature, that He is "*closer to me than I am to myself*", to help find God in the absence of experience, and to confirm that the body recognizes Christ even when the mind doesn't understand.

This was not just a mental insight – the truth of it was *revealed*, expressed and confirmed, assuring me that this was the whole point of the long experience. God had been right there with me showing me this deep truth of Its presence and patiently waiting for me to grasp it. And to further confirm my understanding, after that, the experience never returned! It was as if God said, *I am here, in this Blessed Sacrament, this is the most profound and available place for you to find me – regardless of experiencing it or not experiencing it*.

Could I ever leave the Church when this had been made so evident to me? Never. As Bernadette wrote, "*As Catholics we do not know where God is not, but we do know where God is*". That it took two solid years of this daily experience for me to get it, speaks to God's patient commitment to healing my blindness.

What had been revealed at Barre through experience was now permanently revealed as *no-experience*. God is the Ground of all experience, and the Ground of no experience. Hard to speak about, but beyond doubt.

"Lord, we give what you take and we take what you give."

~*Mother Teresa*

A Dose of Reality

Later, in a letter, I admitted to Bernadette that I did not feel like a Catholic. Though I was no longer practicing Buddhist techniques, I was still sitting daily in meditation, which seemed Buddhist to me. She reminded me that Carmelite nuns have been meditating two to four hours a day for hundreds of years! Bernadette reminded me that, as far as she was concerned, a true Catholic is one who recognizes Christ in the Eucharist.

I could certainly no longer deny that I had that recognition. What had happened at that retreat was that after years of being a *closet Catholic,* I could never again doubt or deny what God had taken such pains to show me. I knew myself to be, Catholic. And happily wanted others to know me as that too.

At the end of the 1998 retreat, before leaving for the airport, I went into the chapel to sit before the Blessed Sacrament in the Tabernacle. The tabernacle is a small ornate box that sits near the altar and has a red light over it. Inside the tabernacle consecrated Hosts to be served in the Mass are kept.

As I sat there, there was the simple sense of just being my plain self and sitting in peace before the Almighty. I felt God, not within this time, but *without*, all around me, a tacit sense of being *in* God. I saw a light streaming out from the Tabernacle and filling the space of the room, raining down like grace on all. I blinked several times but the vision remained.

Even at the airport in Los Angeles this vision continued. I saw all the people there as the impersonal suffering masses, a baby screaming, being ignored by its angry mother, people sitting alone eating bad food, a grown man in a suit with a briefcase obviously terrified of flying. Faceless people wandering, rushing, a feeling of cold chaos.

Everyone seemed locked into their little individual hell, even the smiling ones, the talking ones. But something else was happening; this was not the usual dark view of struggling mankind. It took me a minute to realize what I was seeing which was all of us completely enveloped in God – and ignoring It.

Rich ones, poor ones, cool ones and hip ones, lost and frightened ones, all constantly supported by and taking life from the One without seeming to know it. So beautiful and so sad. Using up our spark of life, a spark that came directly from God, to build our own small fires. Grasping at the possibility of warmth but never feeling the warmth all around us and ignoring the Absolute Fiery Life that is our own existence.

The vision was overwhelming – the equality of all beings in God's eyes regardless of status or class or position in this world. Once you get a glimpse of what It is that is living you now, depending on anything else no longer makes sense. It is not possible to let go however, until you see that you are already held.

Sitting in prayer the next day after arriving home – a sudden vision arose in my mind. A great rolling river, very wide and muddy brown, with flashes of color appearing and disappearing as objects, and even perhaps people, rise to the surface and sink again. The great brown river moved over the land and shaped it, a mighty flood, a thing to behold.

Then from above and to the left of my field of vision poured down a stream of molten gold which, when it touched the river, formed a brilliant stream within it. The river carried the golden stream as it moved along but did not absorb it.

In some places, the golden stream was wide on the back of the river; in other places it dwindled down to a thin thread. Sometimes it flowed close to the shore and formed a pool, sometimes it moved down the center of the river and far from the shore. The river carried the stream and the stream needed the river; they were inexorably connected and vital to each other.

The river is the Church. The golden stream is the mystical Truth within the tradition.

A Chance to Help

As life continued I found myself looking around for some work, something to serve God and others. Was there a way to share what I had been given? In the effort to discover a vocation, we have to follow our deepest heart, go after whatever it is that strengthens our love for God.

Why not try everything, follow every thread and see where it goes. If one road falls apart, accept it and try another. If we are looking for the best place to live or find a vocation we have to go and knock on those doors, ask and find out. I knew I didn't want to just sit around waiting to know the will of God. I decided I would pray about it and if nothing obvious showed itself, then I would just use the experience and the intelligence that God had already given me, and make the best decision I could. If it was not meant to be, it won't happen – or if it does happen it might fall apart, and then reveal the next step.

It may turn out that we must leave everything behind, which is difficult. But to go all the way with

God there must be a willingness to leave everything behind. Progress is entirely in proportion to the ability to drop anything and everything; if you feel the drive to do it, don't waste it.

It is a rare gift. Usually people rationalize or find a way out of dropping everything. This is why the contemplative path does not attract or hold everyone. The path is open to everyone but the courage to follow is a gift.

Our love of God, our determination to know God, and our desire for Truth will give us the courage to follow the path. How it turns out in life is for what you might call the *outer person*. To be a mother or father, or a committed virgin or a solitary, or a monk or nun – all that is the *outer person*.

These things, while not inconsequential, are not of the essence. It is the inner self or what we might call the higher person that God acts on; it is that which is really going to change. God doesn't seem to care what we do outside, as long as it is a moral life, a right or decent life. Aside from that, none of these choices can keep us from God. Ultimately everyone's vocation is to give their life to God, regardless of where or how. Our part in the transformative process is to do everything we can to love and know God. Even if we make a mistake the intention to do something for God will either make it right or God will lead us to know that it is not necessary.

Time and experience (through the Grace of God) taught me that even if I didn't find the right spiritual community or monastery, ultimately it didn't matter. The situation had nothing to do with my real vocation, which was to give my whole life to God, to recognize God as the living center of everything.

Living the contemplative life or give my whole life to God doesn't depend upon the externals of the thing. My real vocation is right here and now – it is not down the road somewhere. We carry our monastery with us. So I set out to put myself in various situations to see where God might be leading.

I had never considered myself to be the type to teach others, it made me uncomfortable to be the one at the front of the room. But, wanting to leave no stone unturned, I tried it out several times. Once I was asked to give a talk on the Ten Ox-Herding pictures[8] to a class of college students.

The thought of standing at the front of a room to give a talk was frightening and I considered refusing the invitation. Then I heard the words in my head: *Go ahead and do it. If you do a good job it will be a useful thing for the students, and if you make a fool of yourself it will be a useful thing for you.* I did it and, indeed, it was partly useful for me and hopefully, partly useful for them. I never, before or since, felt any urge to try to be a teacher or to give talks. Only a calling from God would allow someone to do that as a kind of service to God.

Eventually I quit my office job and joined a volunteer program run by the Franciscans to work for one year at a California Mission. I hoped this would be my chance to serve God and others.

I had the (somewhat romantic) image in my mind of working with the homeless, the sick and the

---

[8] Ancient images used in Zen Buddhist to describe the stages of spiritual practice. (See: Ten Oxherding Pictures by D.T. Suzuki).

poor, but as it turned out, God saw the needy as something entirely different. I visited three different missions to be interviewed by the priests, nuns, lay brothers and staff. It was brought home right away, even during those interviews, that I would be required to put aside my personal preferences and judgment of others if I was to be of any use at all.

The environment of the Missions was nothing like that of convents of cloistered nuns or a monastery full of silent monks. It was much more ordinary, and I had not yet realized the great need to meet God in the ordinary.

Though I had hoped to serve the poor, in the end I was sent to the rich and famous. I met with the priests and the one sister at Serra Retreat, the Franciscan Mission in Malibu, California, and was invited to stay and become part of the staff. I reminded myself that my main reason for joining the Franciscans was to serve, to live the contemplative life and nothing else. I was sorry not to be working directly with the needy, but I determined to just follow where I felt God had led me and do the best I could do.

In Malibu rich folks and movie stars were everywhere; there was not a poor person in sight – except those living in the retreat center! When life goes in a completely different direction from what we had planned, God usually has a hand in it. I accepted the invitation and moved to Malibu.

It was in a beautiful place, on a plateau high above the town with a clear view of the beach and the ocean. Because of the kind of retreats held there, I developed a more realistic impression of the Church, one that was quite different from the rarified and holy atmosphere of monasteries and convents. I was getting a taste of the more conventional view of Catholicism, a kind of *Sunday go ta meetin'*, type of religion, something I did not like and had always avoided.

The retreats were very different from ones I had experienced in Buddhist centers. One amusing example; when attending Buddhist retreats, at the meals, we were usually served brown rice and vegetables, miso soup and tofu – all kinds of nourishing, healthy and, admittedly, trendy foods.

At my first retreat at Serra we were served beanie-weenies! Dinner was roast chicken, white sheet cake and a glass of wine. The retreat rooms were appropriately plain, with a crucifix or picture of Mary on the wall. But the atmosphere was seldom peaceful, much less silent. Endless chatting and socializing, even music for evening dancing on some nights – never before had I seen such a *retreat*. Living at Serra was rather like living in a hotel. There were few nights when the place was not full with people slamming doors and talking in the hallways, even watching loud TV in the next room!

To say it turned me off is an understatement. Sometimes I would go down to the parking area to sit in my car for prayer and reading. I knew I could never leave Christ, but I had hoped I would always be able to find convents and similar holy places to go to Mass. It may be obvious that I felt spiritually superior to nearly everyone there, though no doubt denying that to myself.

Even the priests did not invoke or express reverence, one of them went so far as to make sarcastic comments about people who got down on their knees to receive Communion. This was the side of the Catholic Church I had feared and dreaded. And yet I didn't have to be told it was not my place to criticize, nor would that be of any use.

This kind of scenario was, I was sure, in the minds of my Buddhist friends who criticized the Church and me for joining it. As yet unaware of my spiritual snobbery, I tried to hold myself aloof from the kind of Catholic gatherings I was seeing.

This was the beginning of an important part of the maturation process. My circumstance for the next several years was one in which I would only be able to spend time with *churchy-Catholics* in their *ordinary* spiritual gatherings. It was necessary for me to get past the need to see myself (and God) as somehow above all this, and, instead, find Truth in things *just as they are*.

Without the Eucharist I would have failed. But even here, in this imperfect environment, the Blessed Sacrament was the same powerful, deep connection to

God's presence, regardless of reverence, or the lack of it at any Mass.

I could not know the thoughts of the other Catholics I was meeting, nor their relationship with God. Not everyone wants or needs to be a contemplative. St. Teresa of Avila wrote that all nuns are not contemplatives, nor do they need to be to live their life with God[9]. I was Catholic, yes, but I was identified with Contemplatives (capital C) and monastics, and I felt surely God was too!

In my earlier years, I thought of myself as Buddhist and superior to Catholics, and now here I was again, thinking myself Catholic and superior to *ordinary* Catholics. I did not yet have the wisdom to realize that there is no use replacing one identity with another. I had to just relax and remind myself: *This is the way it is*.

My time at the retreat center came to an end. I knew that my vocation was as a contemplative, but I still had the urge to do something for God and

---

[9] *To Believe in Jesus*, 91.

neighbor. What I didn't see at the time was that this urge to do something special was less about God than a kind of ambition. I was still missing the lesson of simply doing what needs to be done, leaving the rest to God. Still, I often wondered, what is the right work for a contemplative? Perhaps I had some contribution to make, but maybe it would be accomplished without my ever knowing it!

One day, after Mass, as I sat in the chapel, in my mind's eye I saw an empty room with a doorway. A person was seated in the room and another person was on their knees outside the door, looking down the hallway to the left where the *Glory of God* was blazing. The seated person couldn't see down the hall, but they could see the person kneeling in the doorway. That kneeling person's face was diffused with joy and the Glory was shining on them, like light shining into a mirror.

As long as the kneeling person remains absorbed in the Vision, that Glory is also reflected to the one in the room, without the direct view. The person kneeling in the doorway must pay no attention to the

one in the room or to anything else, but only hold res-
olutely to the Vision.

In that way, God can make use of someone
even without their knowing they are helping anyone
else. Whether there is someone in the room watching
or there is no one, that is not the concern of the one
who sees. Their concern is holding the Vision, allowing themselves to be absorbed in it and even when they
no longer see it, to stay focused on the Invisible God. I
understood from this vision that reflecting God's love
to others is God's work; holding and returning to the
vision *is* the work of the contemplative.

Holding the vision in my present circumstance
was still a work in progress. Starved for silence and
solitude, I asked for time off to make a retreat at Mt.
Tabor Monastery, an Eastern Rite Catholic monastery,
a very holy place.

At Mt. Tabor, it seemed to me that the monks'
lives were full of hardship and prayer. How they found
the motivation to attend long services three or four
times each day, services which are sung for the most
part, and sung standing, I could not say. They are

motivated by something stronger than the paltry desire to get enlightenment for themselves.

It was a Zen-like Catholic monastery in the sense that it was very focused and serious, and the community life was mostly in silence and work. Most likely I could have found the same atmosphere in Cistercian and Benedictine monasteries, but I did not know that then. In any case it was a great relief from the parish church atmosphere and showed me yet another side of Catholicism.

While I was there, I bought a beautiful icon of the Theotokos, Mary as the Bearer of God, a smaller version of the big one behind the altar in their Church. It had been painted in the traditional way, even raising the chickens who laid the eggs that went into the tempura paint. The icon artist fasted and prayed, and spent time alone while painting it. To bless the icon, it stayed for a day and night on the altar where the priests prepared the Blessed Sacrament. That icon was to be my traveling companion for many years and hangs on the wall above my head as I write this.

The picture is of a strong, older Mary with the child Jesus on her lap. The gold frame around the figures is penetrated by Mary's halo, her elbow and part of her robe, showing that she breaks the usual framework of human beings by her holiness.

I had to promise the monks that the icon would never be disrespected in any way, nor sold. If I died and did not pass it on to someone who would agree to those terms, the icon should be burned or buried. Perhaps the reverence with which it was painted and then passed to me gave it its special feeling of aliveness. I've learned that the honest prayer of the unbeliever has tremendous power. We can go to Mary, even with our disbelief, for she is real and truly there to help us, and that is a truth for Catholics, non-Catholics, and even non-Christians. I heard about Mary before I joined the Catholic Church. All the fuss made of her was confusing then.

It seemed to me she was an idea needed by those of a sentimental bent, and I knew I was not one of those people. So I just put a question mark after it and went on. This was until I met Mary personally in that miraculous way, during the dark times in Kansas.

Years later I would hear Bernadette Roberts say that when you can't get to God, that is the time to turn to Mary. To this day I do not feel any sentimental love or devotion for Mary. For me, she is the wise, strong Mother, a support in difficult times or periods of deadness and dryness in prayer, who never coddles or expects sentimental feelings. And she is profoundly mystical; still, to this day, I don't know what she could possibly be or how it is that asking Mary to pray for us can have such a powerful effect. I only know that it does, even for the unbeliever. There is a great mystery here, too great for conventional religiosity. If the idea turns anyone off, I would challenge them to think again about Mary.

At the end of my time with the Franciscans, I found out that my brother, who lived in Arkansas, was in a battle with cancer. My year at the retreat center had initiated the process of learning tolerance of others and finding God in the ordinary; now in Arkansas it was to continue and intensify. My family saw me as anything but ordinary.

Life as a professional spiritual seeker had led me into some very exotic circumstances and cut me off from them. They didn't quite know what to make of me or say to me, and so kept me at arm's length for the first months I was there. It was no use trying to explain that wherever I went, I was trying to find God. Even that was strange to them.

I just made an effort to fit in, go unnoticed. I had lived an exotic lifestyle – and loved it – but now, following the Catholic path, this ancient traditional path, was like finding God right there in the place where I stood. As Jacob said, standing at the ladder, *This place is Holy and I knew it not (Gen. 28:16)*. Seeing God in things just as they are, was an awakening of self-acceptance.

In Arkansas I learned a tried and true way out of the mental or emotion disturbances I had experienced in life: go do something for someone else, just for their sake, with, *nothing in it for you*. Forget yourself and the pain is forgotten too. I was learning what the Little Flower called, *monotonous sacrifice*. I had a chance to be there for my brother and his family, whether or not they showed any appreciation.

At first I felt out of place attending daily Mass at the little parish Church, still missing the intellectual give and take experienced in the California Buddhist communities.

I did not know nor did I want to know any of the other people in the Church on those dark mornings. We silently entered, crossed ourselves, genuflected, and sat down to pray, morning after morning. The priest came in and we followed the prescribed order of asking for help and forgiveness, praying for others, listening to words of encouragement, hope and discernment. Then the priest offered the sacrifice of the Mass.

We walked up together, each bringing his or her own inner gift and need, received the Present Truth of the Blessed Sacrament, then returned to our seats and silently gave thanks. Morning after morning.

Though we hardly spoke, I began to recognize certain faces and they seemed to recognize mine. They became for me a silent community of prayer and I began to value it – even more than the intellectual discussions of the past. The Sunday Masses were still difficult – so many people and so much more going on besides prayer and Communion. But I just kept going, strengthened by the Eucharist and figuring God would help me tackle the rest further on. For now I had my first Catholic community and I was grateful. May I suggest that anyone who struggles with what they find at Sunday Mass should try attending the daily Mass. It is an entirely other kind of service.

I was offered the opportunity to take care of an elderly woman, Eileen, who was suffering dementia brought on by a stroke. I agreed to live in her home, and though I still had a full-time job, try to help her and keep her safe.

As I watched her become more and more confused and lost, the most painful thing to see was her family's upset and frustration with the changes in their mother. Eileen was Catholic but her children had stopped taking her to Church because they were afraid of what she might do there. I tried taking her several times and, it was true, she did become confused and anxious.

Her lips would move in time with the old familiar prayers, but she would stand up at the wrong time or speak loudly into the silence. I stopped taking her to Church, nonetheless she still took her rosary to bed every night, and together we would say the Lord's Prayer.

She told me an amazing story about that rosary. In World War II her husband, Paul had been a platoon leader, and his platoon had been dropped behind enemy lines to find and lead other lost soldiers back to safety. The small troop of men, about ten in all, were hiding in the countryside of France, with German soldiers everywhere. Germany had invaded France; everyone was afraid, and with good reason. He and his men were exhausted and hungry and hoping to find a place where they could safely rest for a time. They came to a small farmhouse at the edge of the woods.

As they looked, they saw a woman in the barn, milking a cow, with two small children playing nearby. They knew the woman would be terribly frightened to see them but they were desperate. They had no idea of her sympathies, whether she would even be willing to give refuge to a group of American soldiers.

When they came haltingly out into the clearing she jumped up in great fear and grabbed the children. Her eyes were wide with terror as she looked at them. Paul tried to explain to her that they meant no harm but the woman could not understand them and no one in the group spoke French. She was frozen with fear. What to do? Suddenly an idea came to him. He reached into his pocket, then held his hand out in front of him.

In it was Elaine's small rosary which she had sent with him for protection in the war. The French woman looked down at the rosary, looked up at him and slowly made the sign of the cross. He also made the sign of the cross. She shyly smiled and nodded at him, and motioned him and his men into the barn. The rosary and the silent gesture said everything that needed to be said – they could trust each other. The soldiers hid for two days in the barn and the woman fed them as well as she could until they were ready to go. I still cannot tell this story without being deeply moved. If there is a better example of what true spiritual community is, I don't know it. No wonder the rosary was so precious to her.

Hoping to offer Elaine some of the comfort of her faith I went to the local parish priest to ask if I might become a Eucharistic minister. I was able to take the training and bring Communion to her in the calm environment of her home. It was a comfort to her. On her clearer days she would sometimes become very sorrowful, feeling her life was now worthless and wondering why she had to continue living. When I reminded her that without her I would not have become a Eucharistic minister, she would nod and smile. My time with Eileen set me onto a path I would follow for years after, caring for people with Alzheimer's and other forms of dementia.

People suffering from dementia have lost all memory of themselves and purpose. These people, even though confused and utterly helpless, are obviously still with us, perhaps in part to give us the opportunity to serve others with nothing in it for us.

Through the effort of their own will they cannot grow closer to God, learn or change, or do anything for themselves or anyone else. Yet they were still alive and their lives clearly have an effect on those around them. It seems God is not finished with them in this world, so neither can we toss them aside or hide them in some forgotten facility.

If you want to find the "poorest of the poor" – the most vulnerable of all – look no further. They are more vulnerable than babies because they are no longer sweet or cute, and, for the most part, they are incapable of even acknowledging or responding, even with a smile, for service done for them. Those suffering from dementia are indeed helpless and need much care.

In a few years, I was finally able to retire from administrative work and begin caring full time for others, like my friend Eileen.

While caring for Eileen I continued studying and practicing my new Catholic faith. For much of my life I had been confused about the Christian Way. I believed deeply in God, but Jesus was a big problem.

I could agree that Jesus had lived two-thousand years ago, a model of a God-centered life, and, according to what I was told, Christians could expect to meet this Jesus again in the future, either in heaven or the second coming. The insurmountable question for me, however, was: what about now?

What does the man Jesus have to do with this moment, this instant of consciousness; what is he in our experience, except a memory or an idea – neither of which I had much faith in as a way to know God. The Jesus that those ideas implied was strictly on the *outside*, *other* than consciousness, something separate from my own self, my consciousness. Only as I began to understand the Trinity in an experiential way did I grasp the difference between Jesus and Christ, and come to know the present and eternal Reality of Christ.

There was (and still is) much more to learn, but the understanding that gradually came was like the opening of a door into the deeper level of the Christian revelation than I had known before. It changed everything. Though the words below had not yet been published, they, more than any other, explain what I was coming to understand.

> "In Truth, man's true spiritual life is the Trinity, for what is that in man that knows God? It is the *Logos*. What is that in man that loves God? It is the *Spirit*. What is that in man that sees God? It is the *Transcendent*." [10]

Even before I understood this, for the first time in my life and spiritual journey, I knew I was home. That I didn't fully understand everything was not an obstacle.

In my younger days, I was one of those people who said they didn't need *organized religion* (always

---

[10] *The Real Christ*, Bernadette Roberts, 88.

said with a slight sneer). But with the Blessed Sacrament it is not a matter of going to Mass in order to be a good Catholic, a member of the true Church, or any other such reason.

It is the Thing Itself, that does the work. Regardless of how that sounds, I am as sure of that as I am of my own existence and because of that assurance, there is a strong urge to share it.

One great thing about the Catholic faith is that when you can't understand some piece of doctrine, you just continue going to Mass, practicing, if you will, and these things are usually revealed, if it is necessary for you. True Faith is not dependent on belief. Because of the Eucharist, when there was something I didn't understand or agree with I didn't have to throw the baby out with the bath water. *I am the Way, the Truth and the Life.*

Trusting in this, I continued going to the Sunday Mass in my little Arkansas Church, regardless of my opinion of how they were and how they should be. I recall one particular Sunday when it was *Boy Scout*

Appreciation Day. I thought about not going but decided to go for the Eucharist.

The service was all the things I was least comfortable with, but this time I made a conscious effort to just be present and drop the judgments. When it came time for the sacrifice of the Mass, there again was that happy certitude, and on this day, it was accompanied by feelings of love and peace and even gratitude for all the happy families that were there.

It felt like my final exam in joining the Church and with God's help I passed. I also got a good lesson, which is that if we come to church for the people, or a nice priest or a particularly good homily, that is likely all we will get.

By January 2001 my brother's cancer was in remission so I left Arkansas and returned to California. During the long drive from Arkansas to Our Lady from Mt. Tabor Monastery, the icon sat in the front seat with me.

Childhood Dreams

I returned to live in Santa Rosa, California with an old friend, and found a job working for a local conservation organization. However, symptoms of carpal tunnel made the work difficult and an operation was scheduled.

Recuperating and rehabilitation from the surgery entailed months off work. The doctor told me I would be wise never to take another job that required keyboarding, which pretty much eliminated office jobs. Though I still could not see how typing had been God's work, the light was dawning that this ordinary skill had allowed me many opportunities as well as a safety net for the spiritual search. And now I would be free forever from that kind of work (or so I thought) – but I did not feel relieved.

I couldn't imagine how else I could ever make a living – it was worrying. The hands are all about usefulness, and I felt my usefulness was slipping away from me – another identity to be surrendered. The realities of age and health were beginning to catch up with me.

A certain panic set in as I felt the body beginning to age and fail. It was like discovering a leak in your boat out on the ocean. Strength of body and personal energy had been my rod and my staff, and I could see a time down the road when these things might be removed from me.

At times I still experienced a grinding feeling of inner restlessness, telling me that I was not where I wanted or perhaps should be. There was still that old inner agitation that would not be still. *Our hearts are restless until they rest in Thee.* For years, I had been tormented by this restlessness, the sense of something wanting or incomplete.

The sensation was almost physical, an uncomfortable *twitchy* feeling that I was not doing the best thing, or that I needed to go to another place, to a different situation, intensify my life or simplify my life. The ever-present gnawing ate away at me, even keeping me awake some nights.

Ultimately, I discovered that this feeling really has nothing to do with lifestyle, where we live, who we live with, our job, or anything else. The truth is, I could have been in a monastery or a hermit cave and it wouldn't have changed a thing.

Consciousness itself gives rise to a certain undefined restlessness in us – as if we know there is more to existence than this earthly life, more to us than what we believe ourselves to be.

Consciousness is so vast and so mysterious that we feel it must either *be* divine, or be an opening into the divine. Restlessness is caused by the fact that consciousness never completely reveals or completely hides the Truth, it only veils it, leaving us with a longing that seems to come from our very core.

I thought perhaps I might have to live with this gnawing incompleteness for the rest of my life, knowing it may just be a cross to bear. I decided to try one last time to find and make a life commitment before giving up. There was no better time to attempt to follow through on my childhood desire to enter the Carmelites.

I contacted a Carmelite convent and applied to be an extern sister. An extern sister is not cloistered as are the nuns, but lives just outside the convent and lives a life of service to God by caring for the nuns and guests.

I began a correspondence with the Mother Superior of the community, and frequently visited her to discuss the possibility of entering. I knew I was pretty old to be accepted and, considering my age and health problems the chances were not good. In fact, in retrospect, it was probably a foolish idea. But it was a desire that had played on the edges of my mind all my life; this was a circling back around to that childhood wish, and an expression of my intent and commitment to living life with God. So I made application.

The interviews with the Mother Superior gave me hope as she confirmed the spirit of Carmel in me. I felt most at home in silence, solitude and community, but God does not always send us where we feel most at home, asking us instead to find God wherever we call home.

I was applying to be a Carmelite while I had to admit I still did not fully understand Christ nor Christianity, much less Jesus. But by then that seemed like a wonderful problem. Thanks to the writings of Bernadette and a few others, I knew a great deal more than before about Christ and Christianity and anyway, had accepted that we can never know God fully, face-to-face, in this life.

I felt I was working on the *koan* Jesus gave to Peter: *But you, who do you say that I am?* Answering that is the work of a lifetime. I knew Christ's true presence in the Eucharist. I knew God was closer to us than we are to ourselves, closer than our breath. The rest would come.

In the Carmelite interviews I confessed (and not the first time) to a very wild early life. I had been married, then divorced and then lived the hippy lifestyle for some years, behaving in ways that still pained me to remember. I had lived my life at that time, for experience and for what I could get out of life and out of others.

Before my conversion, when guilt would strike, I tried to make light of my own sins by looking at the world and comparing myself to others, thinking myself no worse, as if sins are relative to others and not to God. I did my best to be totally honest with the Mother Superior and prayed for the right outcome.

A few weeks later I received a letter saying the Carmelites had turned me down. The Mother Superior said that though I did have the spirit of Carmel, my age and health prohibited them from accepting me, even as an extern. She said that in the old days they would most certainly have taken me but now most of their sisters were quite elderly, and there were only a few still young enough to assist them. They no longer receive enough financial support to allow them to take anyone in who requests it, even those with a vocation. There was nothing I could do but accept the decision, though now not being able to enter religious life and having to stay *in the world,* gave me once again that feeling of a door being closed.

This time however, the door to God had already been opened and would stay open. I joined a group of

Discalced Carmelite Oblates or Seculars, women and men living the Carmelite charism in the world. Then, just to make double-sure my place wasn't in a religious order, I made a rather half-hearted attempt to enter the Dominicans, which also failed. So I was back with the question: Could I make use of the crazy life I had lived, did it have a purpose? I felt that it did because as Sister Ruth Burrows wrote, *Each life is a history of salvation written by God.*[11]

During the following years life brought many difficult situations, including having to move several times, living on the financial edge, including a period of homelessness, and more travel, including a trip back to Kansas to care for my son after a bad automobile accident. I continued my work with the vulnerable elderly, now four days a week, and attended daily Mass. Living without the search for God as my *be-all and end-all* was surprising, a bit like free falling, as if I had been pressing against a door with all my strength – and the door suddenly opened.

---

[11] *Before the Living God.*

Hunting through spiritual books, the desire for spiritual experiences, long retreats and urgent prayers to know God – all these had fallen away. I had not realized how much time and attention these things had taken, until these activities were no longer needed, nor possible. Just as when I walked down the Church isle after Communion those years ago, I was just my plain self – and God was right there, though *unseen, unfelt.*

It was now possible to simply turn from self-concern and problems in the mind, and see them for what they are – just thoughts, just feelings – in a word, powerless.

I did take a few forays back into the Buddhist community, once even making a trip to the Zen Center where I had previously lived at the request of a visiting friend who practiced Zen. The impressions: Sweet smell of grass and weeds roasting the hot sun; screeching cicadas, chant sounds drifting through the sun and shade, Manzanita bushes, red limbs scaling, prayer flags listless, a brief faint lift from a small breeze. Hunching up the hill beneath the unblinking gaze of the sun, with nothing in our minds but shade.

The Zendo, aromatic with years of incense and wood wax, perfect, subtle decorations of dried leaves and lotus pods.

Yes, it did cause me to remember the lovely, solemn dance of Zen form, the silence in, through and around everything, and sometimes the plain grubbiness of it. Dirty feet beneath graceful black robes, oatmeal in the morning and tofu with spinach at lunch. I liked remembering the person I appeared to be there, wearing Japanese robes with the best of them – all the Kansas covered up. Overcoming the body's complaint at the pre-dawn rise and run. Especially sweet, that black robed Zen identity.

I was thought to be a serious practitioner because I was one of the residents, and because I did the practice with much zeal. It gave me a sense of self I was proud of. Then God took it all apart again, relieved me of it. Now visiting the Center was like going to a place where I once had a lovely vacation. It generated no desire to return. Though I will always feel a strong respect and love for Zen, it no longer had spiritual value to me.

Near the End

In 2008 I began managing the blog site of Bernadette Roberts,[12] a site created to make her books and tapes more readily available. Through that work I heard from others who, like myself, came to Catholicism through a circuitous route and so I began to think it might be good to write about my own journey. Bernadette frequently encouraged her friends to write their own stories. For the sake of authenticity, she suggested writing it, then going through and removing everything about her. That way it would be my own story, what God did in my life.

I had been asked to do this writing a number of times by friends and now, as I was aging, I felt I'd better do it while I still remembered it. When I first sat down to write, I wasn't sure there was enough of a story, so I structured the manuscript around letters to and from friends, between Bernadette and myself, and notes from retreats.

---

[12] BernadetteRoberts.blogspot.com.

I told Bernadette about my attempts to write my story and asked about using her letters. She made it clear that anyone who describes their story as being guided and led by another person is making a big mistake.

God is the guide though we often don't see it that way. I certainly didn't at first. I went back to the manuscript and removed the letters and notes, while still giving credit to the various influences, then started over telling how it actually unfolded. As I did this, the Invisible Guide, there from the beginning, stood out. Though I started out believing. It was about the journey to God, now I know that God *was* the journey.

All through the years I kept a journal of significant quotations which I read on a daily basis. I considered it so valuable that I once thought if there were ever a fire, it would be one of the things I would grab before leaving.

In 2014, I had the idea of sharing those quotations with others in the Contemplative Day Book[13]

---

[13]ContemplativeDayBook.blogspot.com.

blog site. Posting to the site also gave me a chance to share stories, insights, lessons and examples of God's grace with others on the path – the kind of sharing that is the essence of spiritual community. The Day Book postings continue, and I am grateful for the opportunity.

Perhaps this story will leave some readers with questions. One question I have already been asked is, did I ever resolve the *Jesus problem*. Once I had an understanding of Christ, I sort of gave up on how to think of Jesus, thinking of it as one of those things that will be revealed in practicing the Way.

Then it came to me that I had one very good option open to me – I could do what Jesus did – love God with all my heart, mind and life. Jesus did not have Jesus; he had God, and so do I and so do you. I still pray to fully understand and relate to the man Jesus. I see him now as an icon of God, someone who lived his whole life in oneness with God's will, who came to bring us the living message of our potential to share in Christ's divinity, the potential of eternal life in Christ. When I see him on the Cross, I remember that ours is not a God who saves us from things; ours is a God that goes through things with us.

Another question asked by friends who did the reading and review of an earlier draft of the story was this: *How is your life different now that you know one-ness with God?* At first life and consciousness were startlingly, amazingly different, because I could so easily compare it with how things were before. But over time, it just becomes ordinary consciousness. There is, however, the awareness that your life does not stop with you, that is open-ended into Something Other.

The *Background* of my childhood experiences is now the present Ground of each moment. Whatever happens, there is an always-present resort, so that feelings, thoughts and problems can be simply turned from, allowing them to fade on their own, and allowing life to be lived just as it is.

This forgetting of self turns out to be surrendering to God's will, to life just as it is. Best of all, I have no problems! Can you imagine saying that? But it is true. I have no problems. Everything clearly comes and goes – except for One Thing. And so I am at peace. It is better than the enlightenment I had in mind in the beginning, but it feels absolutely nothing like what I could call *my realization*. It seems more like what St. John the Baptist said, as God increases, I decrease.

I found my home in the Christian faith and perhaps there are some who wonder why bother with a traditional religion at all? That is certainly a popular point of view these days. With so much material available now, the tendency is to just read from all the traditions, pick something from list A, something from list B, etc., and make up our own tradition – the religion of ME. The problem with this is that most of us start practicing from the point of view of the ego, which, by its very nature, wants what it thinks is best *for it*. When it gets a taste of the boredom, doubt and discomfort that are essential to real spiritual practice, the egoic self cannot help but think that these things are the signs of having gone the wrong way.

Without a traditional guide we will not go through the self-emptying (kenosis) that is absolutely necessary for true spiritual growth. We just won't do it, or we'll do it in such a way that it serves us and not

God. The traditions are the solidification of the experiences of its mystics and true practitioners.

It is like the shell of a snail. The snail's life and experience creates its shell; the shell is made up of the materials of its life, now made solid and visible. This petrified experience is not to be put on in place of our own direct experience, but it is a reminder, a sign of what happened once, to someone, and is still possible.

It is important, however, not to adopt the tradition in such a way as to give up the intensity of your own search; this is a lesson I've personally had to learn again and again. But it is a path someone else has made that you can use when your path *looks like lost*, and you don't know which way to go.

There are secrets to be found imbedded and locked in that path, put there by mystics in the past, which only faith and obedience can open. Commitment to the path will hold you in place during the inevitable times when God's work in you leaves you unable to use your own power.

The promise of this story has been to speak to how I became (and perhaps more importantly, stayed)

Catholic, and how I moved from Eastern practices to full faith and participation in the body of Christ. Essentially the story of *that* journey ends here.

Through the Grace of God, and some rough but necessary lessons, there was no more fence-sitting. Everything that happened after this point happened to a Christian contemplative. Seventy-one years is a long time and many things occurred that are not included in these pages.

I did not share all the stories of my life, but tried to keep the focus on the issue of the path to conversion and then to commitment. If there are unanswered questions or stated opinions and points of view with which not everyone will agree, so be it.

This is just my story. Obviously, I am not theologically astute or a great writer like Thomas Merton or Bernadette Roberts. The story I tell is just as it happened for me. My desire has been to give you the best that was given to me. Any usefulness this story might have for you will be up to God.

I hope, most of all, that I have written about the truth that (1) God IS and (2) God desires to be known.

It has always seemed to me that we are born with all the tools needed for finding God. The mystery of consciousness contains everything we need to find God – except God's Grace, which is always available – in response to our response. The desire to know the Real Truth was my deepest motivation. I got a little bound up for a while in the desire for enlightenment, which for me was the desire to end suffering, have great and mysterious experiences and to understand life.

Fortunately, I was saved from all that by Truth Itself. Even when we are confused or seem to have gone the wrong way, God responds with help. I learned to see beyond my suffering and even beyond mystery, to *what is,* where God Is. It led me to Christ and to the Church.

The books I read, I would say especially those of Bernadette Roberts, provided a bridge out of Eastern practices and into the mystical heart of Christianity. Sometimes those books answered questions and sometimes raised new ones. Though they had a great influence on me it was clear that I had to find answers that were true to my own understanding, which was something I could only find out in my own life with God.

Thank you for reading. God bless us all.

Epilogue

Due to long years of being a bad example, I feel myself specially placed to speak to the peril of following a *famous* spiritual person. Fame is a fate that a truly spiritual person would not choose, something of an oxymoron, perhaps particularly for Christians. It has been my (and their) good and bad fortune to have close contact with quite a few well-known writers and spiritual teachers, including those mentioned in this book.

Additionally, I spent ten years living with a guru in what I now realize was a cult, though at the time, I knew it only as a spiritual community. I now understand my attraction to these people. When you are starting out with an urge to do something about which you know little, you look to the experts – it is natural. In Kansas, what did I have but books and the occasional visiting teacher? Many years were spent trying to sort through books and other sources of information to find the right teacher or tradition. Part of that search was given over to trying to find something with which I could resonate, something familiar enough to recognize, yet also pointing far beyond to the un-known.

An author may write a book containing the ab-solutely best and most important teaching, the *secret of the universe*, but if it is too far from your own experi-ence you won't recognize it. The way of the beginner is to follow your own heart, what calls to you, and that way of the beginner is wise all the way to the end. However, this initial response often becomes lost as we go along.

We meet some extremely charismatic speaker or teacher and find ourselves fascinated and open to what they have to say. It may lead us in a new way – which is not always bad.

I've found that when my path seems to diverge from where I was expecting it to go, God has a hand in it. But if you find that you are going against what your own intuition is telling you, it is important and valua-ble to stop and give that hesitation some attention. The Dalai Lama is quoted as saying it is not too much to watch a teacher for ten years before following them.

In the early days of my own spiritual seeking I first turned to Ramakrishna and his organization, the Vedanta Society, primarily because Ramakrishna's books were some of the ones that made their way to bookstores in Kansas. It was the 1960's and we were becoming more familiar with Hindu spirituality. Ramakrishna was a name I had heard. I had no personal contact with him (I think he might have been dead by then), or with his people, but I learned what I could through the correspondence course they sent me, and then drifted off into other things closer at hand.

Friends in college were transcendental meditators. So in becoming initiated into that practice, I was more or less just following my friends. It was clear to me, even then, that Transcendental Meditation (TM) was a beginner's practice, not something to stay with for years (although, surprisingly, some of my friends did stay for years!).

I met Maharishi when he came to California. Some years earlier I met Satchadananda, a well-known Hindu Yogi who came to my town to give talks and instructions. I saw the adulation of the crowd around both these teachers and though I was drawn to be part of something like that, I was of two minds about it. For one thing, as I said, I wanted to be part of the group doing this cool, exotic thing with someone from a foreign country.

But the second reason was to fulfill an inner urge to be in a situation and doing a practice (meditation) wherein I could come to know the Presence that had introduced itself to me at such a young age. It was characteristic of me to hide my true spiritual intention from others, to mimic their behavior while also having my own agenda.

Eventually I disassociated myself from the TM movement. I continued to meditate but was no longer interested in learning other TM techniques or being part of the organization. I returned to almost constant reading about Eastern traditions and practices.

I was drawn to books on Buddhism, especially those from the Theravada branch of Buddhism, and later, to Zen. There was not much chance of meeting someone from those traditions in Wichita, Kansas, so

I had to be satisfied with what I could learn from books.

At that time, there were no readily available recordings of teachers giving talks. I was attending the local university so I was able to check out quite a few books, though again, in Kansas, the selection was limited. At home I set up an altar and taught myself to meditate as suggested in the Buddhist readings.

Some years after that I had my first real contact with a *spiritual celebrity*, a man known at that time as Franklin Jones, who later became Bubba Free John and eventually Adi Da Samraj. As I tell in my memoir, I found his first book (*The Knee of Listening*) and rather quickly began corresponding with him through one of his close followers.

I made the decision to move to California and live in his community. He was certainly not *world-famous*, but the fact that I had found his book in the University library and the bookstore, and that he had a community around him, said something. What it said was that there were others who believed what this man had to say enough to change their lives.

Again, I was following the followers. This behavior has gotten me into trouble more times than once, as my memoir details. I was not altogether sure what a guru actually was, but I was interested in having the opportunity to talk with and question people who were trying to live a spiritual life.

As I said in *Buddhist to Catholic*, I lived in that community, very close to the guru, for ten years. I can speak personally to his outrageous behavior and abuse of his followers, and even more to the point, to what it is to put your personal values and morals on hold to please the teacher and bow to the pressure of his community. In this situation, more than any other in my life, I drifted quite far from my personal will to know God.

Why was that? Da Free John was certainly charismatic, a powerful speaker who never used notes, who could be very funny, insightful and charming, and who seemed to know us so well that it seemed as if he had some kind of psychic ability. He once made the remark that he didn't need to be psychic to know what we were up to, implying our problems were self-evident.

He just needed to pay close attention, which, by his estimation, few of us were doing. I saw him do things which seemed unexplainable, miraculous, and had experiences while around him that left me sure they had somehow come from him.

Living with the guru was something like watching a good magician. He may do all kinds of strange and unreasonable things, and ask you to do surprising things as well, and you do it because your attention is focused on the outcome, the *trick*. What will he make out of all of this? After some shocking event Da Free John would, almost without exception, gather us together to explain the *teaching* we were being given by what he had done.

This teaching method gave us the reason we needed to stand by without interference or comment while he humiliated or abused someone, or had what was plainly a temper tantrum or episode of drama.

What was he teaching us? Over time this became what it was to be a good devotee, to put up with anything because we believed we would be taught by it. Additionally, in a close-knit group of some five-hundred people who are almost all behaving with an attitude of adoration toward someone or something, you keep your doubts hidden. If other devotees don't blink an eye at abuse, you don't either (at least, I didn't, and I never saw anyone else who did either) even though it may raise grave doubts within you. Little by little you put those grave doubts way down deep. To further justify it, you call your reactions of fear and shock at his behavior, a sign of your own spiritual im-maturity.

When someone leaves the community (especially long-timers and those close to the guru and his inner circle) no one will speak to that person again lest they themselves are forced to take a look at their own doubts. That is how it was for me when I left. To friends and loved ones with whom I had been close for ten years, I may as well have died – actually, I think they would have preferred that.

Only one person had the courage to come and speak to me afterward, and it was obvious that she was in terror the whole time she was with me. A year later I ran into a man I had known in the community, who was still living there, and he told me that it made a strong impression on him when I left. That was because I had been there for a decade and because I was close to the guru and his household. I had responsibilities in the community and was considered a leader.

I had been a missionary, sent around the world to start new communities and teach the way of Da Free John. After leaving, the rumor was spread around the community that I left because I was too worldly and I wanted to go live the wild life. Nothing was further from the truth. What really happened was that I had realized that I could no longer access my personal discrimination and my own will. I had tried to put something between God and myself and, in an act of grace, God called me out. Life in the community was no longer serving God's purpose and therefore, also not mine either.

Once on my own, I continued to meet and, in some cases, become friends with well-known spiritual people. Perhaps it was only because of living at that time in California, where many of these people were located. However, another reason was that, having lived with someone who called himself the Incarnation of God I found it hard to be overly impressed with ordinary humans, no matter their fame. I am grateful to have met them and especially grateful to Jack Kornfield for the help and advice that he gave me. However, I was through with gurus and spiritual teachers, I knew that – though I didn't know how completely that was true.

No human being I met had as powerful an influence on me as Bernadette Roberts. Her authentic experience of God and the gift she has for writing about it spoke strongly to me. I met her at a time when I was already considering Christianity, though mostly (as I say in the book) as the way to understand and quiet the archetypal Christian voices within, voices, ideals and a cosmology which works below consciousness in most of us born in the West. In my experience over the twenty-five plus years I have known her, I have heard Bernadette constantly remind people that she is not a teacher, and they cannot follow her. In her own words:

"Fortunately, in Christianity we have no guru or master set-up – such as found in Hinduism and Buddhism. The reason for this is that absolutely no one can teach another love of God – which is the only thing that makes the journey go. Without this, one is only on a psychological trip. Anyone who gives his life to God will be drawn along like a magnet, God teaching him everything he needs to know along the way, this is how it goes. While the Christian journey is provided with a plethora of books on the subject – accounts given down the centuries – yet, for everyone, it is himself and God alone. …God leads people differently, and one can only be true to God's leading them – and not true to what someone else says. While all are going in the same direction toward the same end, along the way all that is commonly shared is the same Faith and the same common practice of this Faith. Though certainly encouraged and inspired by others, one is always completely on his own, alone with God. To have the slightest dependency on anyone or anything else is to go nowhere. With scathing self-honesty all man can do is constantly face God alone."[14]

I think of Bernadette as something of an *anti-guru*, the antithesis of the *spiritual teacher* model. She is a deeply private person; wanting only to describe her

---

[14] Bernadette Roberts, *Forcing-the-Fit, "A Case of Plagiarism"*, 117.

experience and what God revealed to her through that experience.

In books and retreats she continually insists on the absolute necessity of honesty and authenticity for everyone – there is just no other way to the Truth. I had to struggle against years of wrong thinking to keep free from the tendency to want to follow someone else, and I have had to correct and insist that others understand that Bernadette is truly not my teacher. Everything is our teacher if we are open to it; God uses everything in our favor because everything is God's.

Below I have summarized the problems of a follower, as I found them and struggled with them.

1). You compare yourself with the teacher or realizer, with their understanding and the milestones on their own journey. Sometimes you even try to re-write your own story (in your mind or elsewhere) to fit into their paradigm.

2). You allow their truth to be your truth, even if it is not verified in your own experience. By assuming it unquestioningly you stop your own journey.

3). You turn their story and writing into your rhetoric or dogma. As the traditional Zen aphorism says, the finger pointing at the moon is not the moon. Stare at the finger pointing to the moon, and you'll miss the moon. God may draw you in an entirely different way and because it does not match that of the person you have chosen to follow, you question yourself and God.

4). You try to capitalize on being associated with the leader, glamorized by what they know and have done. You want to be associated with them and seem wise by association, all in service to the ego.

5). The teacher becomes the measurement by which you judge your own relationship with God, thereby not noticing or responding to the direction in which God may be leading you because it does not fit into the paradigm you have assumed.

6). You dismiss all other books, information and people that seem to be in disagreement or at least not fully in line with the person you have chosen to follow. At worst, those who disagree with your teacher become your enemies.

7). By giving the impression to others that your chosen leader has followers, you cause others to also want to become a follower, creating even more trouble for the person you admire, at least if 'followers' are the last thing they want.

8). If your leader goes in a new or unexpected direction it can be confusing. If this change causes you not to follow any longer, you may throw out the baby with the bathwater. Many of those who left DFJ left spiritual practice altogether. Many cradle Catholics who became unhappy with the Church now claim all spiritual or religious life is useless and foolish. On my living room wall is framed embroidery that summarizes the issue, in lines from Basho, a Zen poet:

Do not follow in the footsteps of the wise;
seek what they sought.

God guides your path.

Pax Christi.

A Note from Bernadette Roberts

"I have read your account a number of times. The first impression is that you were blessed (almost predestined) as a youngster in that you came upon God and the quest for Truth by yourself, with no help from family, friends or education. It does seem however, that sitting in the Franciscan monastery field and passing the Carmelite cloister on your way to school might have sparked interest and curiosity, a subtle influence, in other words. That you did not follow up on this, but instead went in search of the Eastern religions is a mystery to me. But it is too late to speculate about that. Regarding your becoming a Catholic, it seems to me you have made a good fit. In fact, you probably should have been one all along, maybe you were! A true Catholic is someone who recognizes Christ in the Eucharist. Absolutely, your good account should be published!"

– Bernadette Roberts

Made in the USA
Middletown, DE
01 September 2023

37803758R00096

On this day

11 years ago

 **Thomas Jackson**
Apr 30, 2012 · 🌐

Kids dont believe everything
you read on Facebook
niggas be lyin lol

On this day
5 years ago

Thomas Jackson   ...
Apr 26, 2018 · 🌐

R.kelly should move to Mars
tonight, in the middle of the
night.

Thomas Jackson

Oct 9, 2021 · 🌐

I was picking up Tj the other day from school and somebody's momma was playing Freaky tales hella loud

On this day
11 years ago

 **Thomas Jackson**
Apr 30, 2012 · 🌐

•••

Just heard a construction worker tell
another construction worker "its to early to
be actin like a bitch" haaaaaa

Just had the worst click the link in my bio experience ever, They need to ban this n#gga from earth.

12 years ago

 Thomas Jackson
Apr 30, 2011 · 🌐

some dude at the mall called me by my real name i got into a karate fighting stance

Thomas Jackson

Nov 2, 2022 · 🌐

This fool said you on songs with snoop, the real snoop not some nigga named snoop from Vacaville 😂😂😂😂😂

On this day
5 years ago

 **Thomas Jackson**
Apr 26, 2018 · 🌐

Just watched Beyoncés old boyfriend talking about why he broke up with her 😂 bro if you would of just held on a lil Longer you would be the new Stedman now you at Ross in the big and tall section 🤦🏿‍♂️

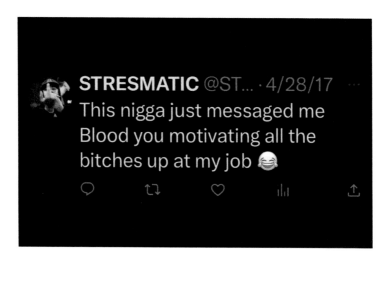

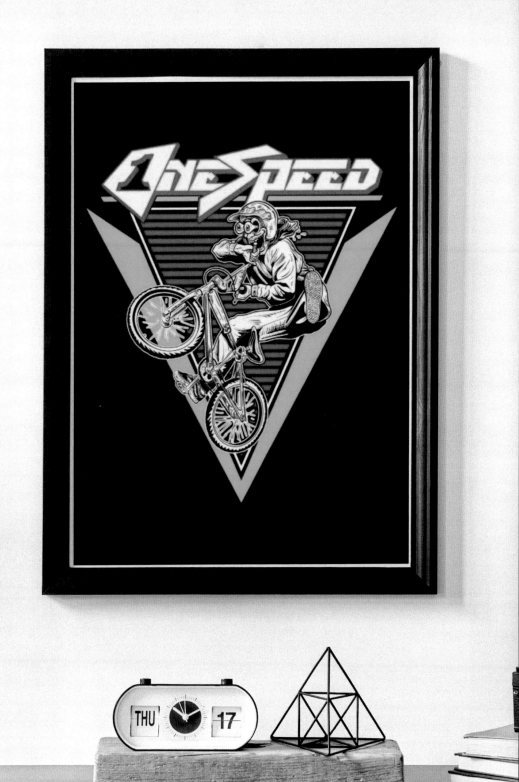

On this day
6 years ago

 **Thomas Jackson**   •••
May 7, 2017 · 🌐

I'm down to go camping if I
can go to a hotel at night lol

People be on here acting like if you drink sea moss you will be able to dunk lol

On this day
7 years ago

 **Thomas Jackson**   ...
May 8, 2016 · 🌐

Terrance Howard's singing
is creepy.

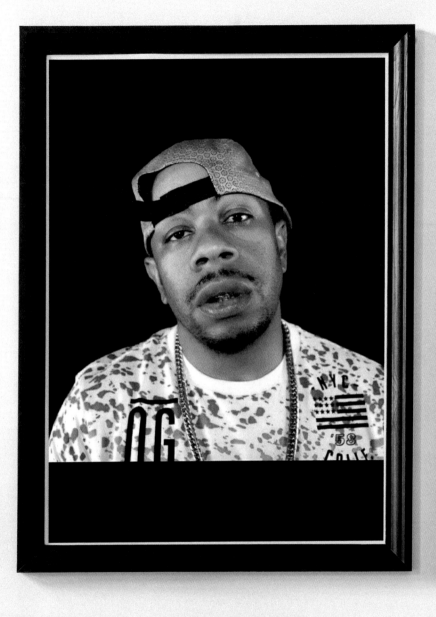

STRESMATIC @... · 10/27/22

When them Yeezys hit Ross and Burlington I'll Be ready.

 1

STRESMATIC @S... · 9/16/19 ···

I'm a regular nigga you might see me in the same fit 20 times

STRESMATIC @S... · 9/16/19 ···
I'm a millionaire in the dollar store

STRESMATIC @S... · 9/13/19 ...
Dear, customer care
representative we ain't friends
bruh just fix the problem my
nigga stop laughing

In Loving Memory

Parvez Altaf Ali

April 20, 1974 to *September 6, 2018*

STRESMATIC @S... · 9/12/19

Walmart is just like Compton

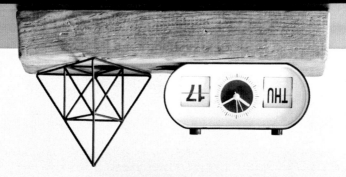

STRESMATIC @S... · 9/28/18

Somebody momma up here stupid thick sheesh 😂😂😂

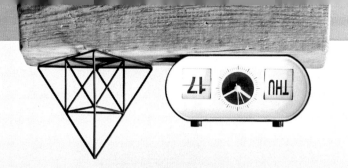

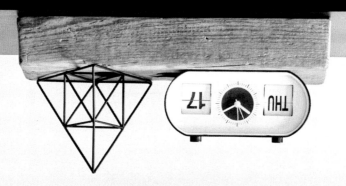

STRESMATIC @S... · 8/22/18

I think chingy hit the wrong weed.

STRESMATIC @S... · 8/21/18 ...

America is definitely putting something in the food because more and more of these broads looking like grown niggas.

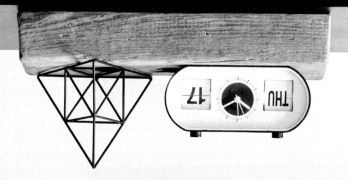

STRESMATIC @S... · 6/15/18

You look like a hater in ya profile pic bro

1

STRESMATIC @ST... · 5/11/18 ···
Someone asked me if I'm
scared of serial killers and stuff
when I ride alone, Hell naw a
serial killer will see me and be
like welp guess I won't be killing
anybody today lol

◯　　　⟳ 1　　　♡　　　ᐟᥱ　　　⬆

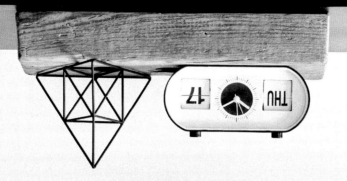

STRESMATIC @S... · 4/26/18 ···
Ain't nothing wrong wit Kanye
that nigga bored

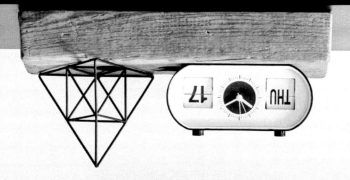

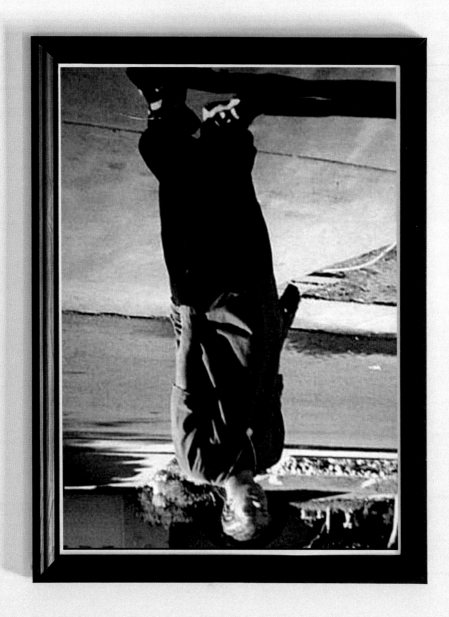

STRESMATIC @S... · 4/25/18 ···

I always answer the front door
holding a gun just in case the
guy selling cleaning products
wanna have a change of plans.

○   ↑⏎   ♡¹   ılı   ↥

STRESMATIC @ST... · 1/23/18

I googled myself one day and it said I had a song with Micheal Jackson 😂

💬   🔁 1   ♡ 1   📊   ⬆

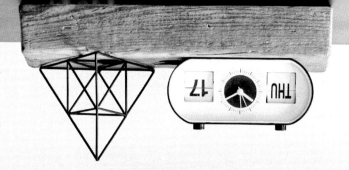

STRESMATIC @ST... · 10/17/17

Solange is light weight fine if Beyoncé ain't around 🖤

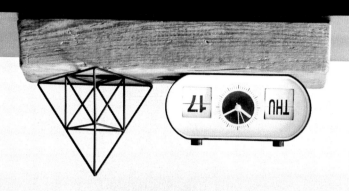

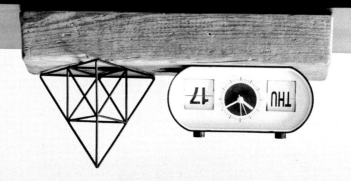

STRESMATIC @ST... · 9/25/17

Lil kids be musty

STRESMATIC @STR... · 9/6/17 ···

A girl told me all rappers do is lick they lips to get ready to lie and text you wyd 😂😂😂

💬   🔁   ♡ 1   📊   ⬆️

STRESMATIC @STR.... · 8/9/17 ···

Just remember when some
money and success comes some
weird niggas will show up and try
to mess it up 😤

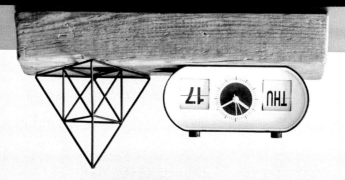

STRESMATIC @ST... · 7/19/17 ···

I stopped fuckin with this girl
because she told me her mom
was a gang member wait what
I'm coo 😵

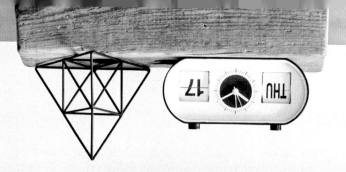

STRESMATIC @ST... · 7/19/17

When a full grown man tells you to follow back nigga why

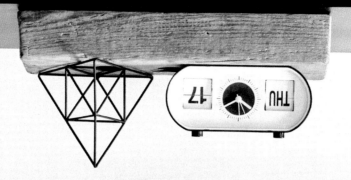

STRESMATIC @ST... · 7/18/17

Rkellys cult member that was on tmz is kinda bad 😂

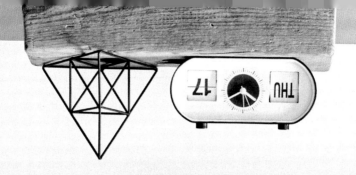

N# GGAS WATCH A
COUPLE YOUTUBE
TUTORIALS ABOUT THE
MUSIC INDUSTRY AND
THINK THEY PUFFY.
-MATIC

I saw a guy I know
hand his cellphone to
his girl in front of me
I felt like melting like
the witch In wizard of
Oz 😂😂😂

When I drop my book I'm
gonna start wearing hella
cologne and church
clothes.

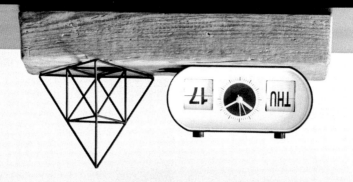

My potna called me the other day and said he's tired of working, And then he says he wishes he could meet a older white woman so he can stay at home all day and eat up all the snacks be on the game watch tv and relax while she's at work 😂😂😂 😂😂😂

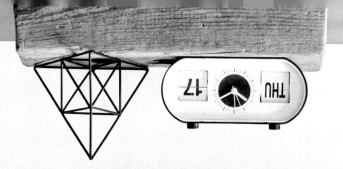

Don't be fooled she might fine in pictures ,but her driver side window probably doesn't roll down.

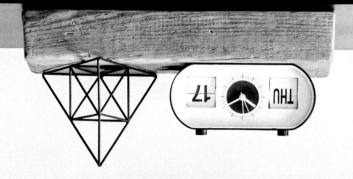

A full grown man with a
beard that connects Dm me
why did you unfollow big
bro ?

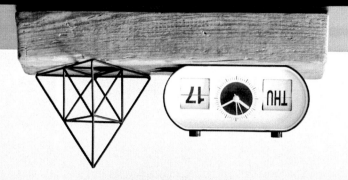
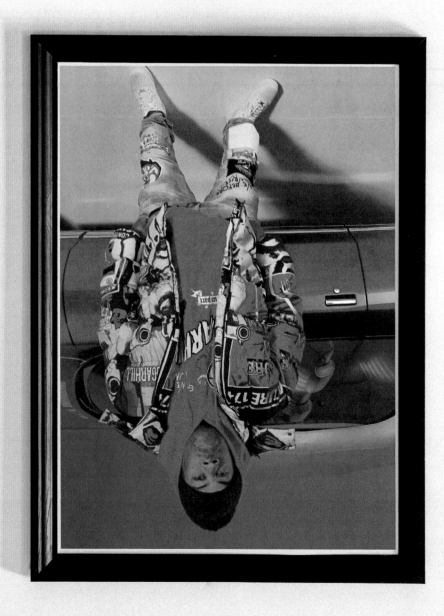

Doja Cats Boyfriend probably always has a headache 😂😂😂

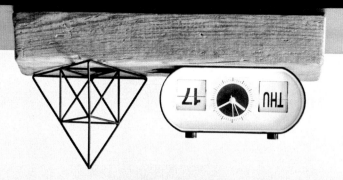
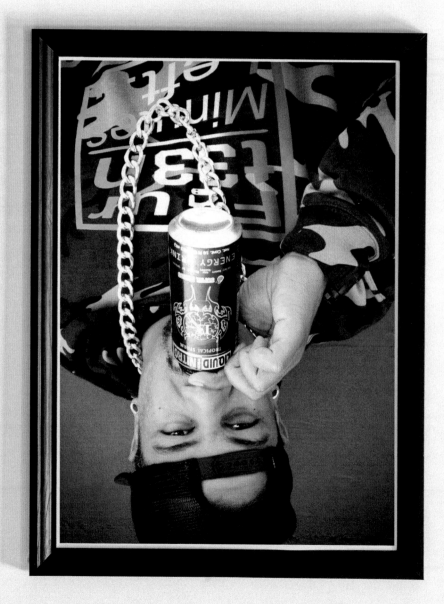

I'm sure some weirdo is sending a AI woman his whole check 🙄🙄

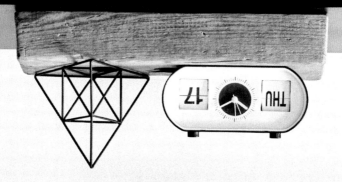

You Hella Stupid Blood

By Rapper/ Song Writer

Thomas "Stresmatic" Jackson

Made in the USA
Middletown, DE
14 August 2023